See Yourself as God Se

San Diego Christian College
Library
Santee, CA

248.4
M138s

SEE YOURSELF

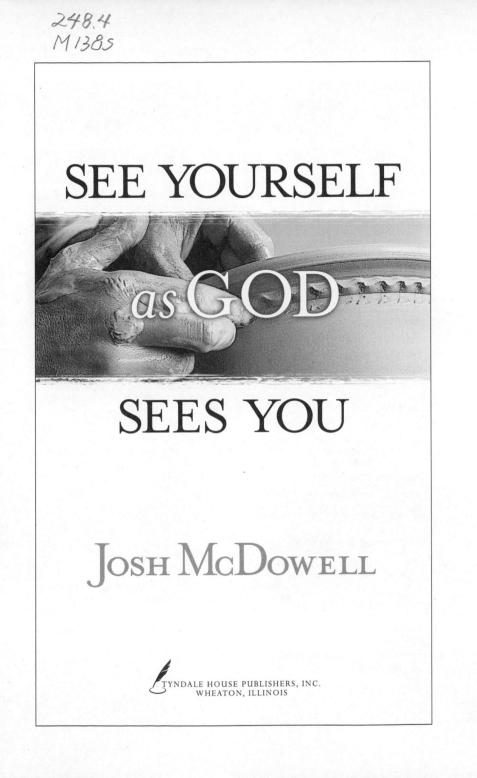

as GOD

SEES YOU

JOSH McDOWELL

TYNDALE HOUSE PUBLISHERS, INC.
WHEATON, ILLINOIS

Visit Tyndale's exciting Web site at www.tyndale.com

Copyright © 1999 by Josh McDowell

All rights reserved.

Cover art copyright © 1999 by Alan Goldsmith/The Stock Market. All rights reserved.

Unless otherwise indicated, all Scripture quotations are taken from the *Holy Bible,* New International Version®. NIV®. Copyright © 1973, 1978, 1984 by International Bible Society. Used by permission of Zondervan Publishing House. All rights reserved.

Scripture quotations marked KJV are taken from the *Holy Bible,* King James Version.

Scripture quotations marked NLT are taken from the *Holy Bible,* New Living Translation, copyright © 1996. Used by permission of Tyndale House Publishers, Inc., Wheaton, Illinois 60189. All rights reserved.

Designed by Justin Ahrens

Edited by Lynn Vanderzalm

Library of Congress Cataloging-in-Publication Data

McDowell, Josh.
   See yourself as God sees you / Josh McDowell.
      p.   cm.
   Rev. ed. of: His image, my image.   1993.
   ISBN 0-8423-1832-1 (sc : alk. paper)
   1. Self-esteem—Religious aspects—Christianity.   2. Identity (Psychology)—Religious aspects—Christianity.   I. McDowell, Josh.   His image, my image.   II. Title.
BV4598.24.M34   1999
248.4—dc21   99-22146

ISBN 0-8423-1832-1

Printed in the United States of America

05   04   03   02   01   00   99

8   7   6   5   4   3   2

CONTENTS

ACKNOWLEDGMENTS

This book is a revision of my previous written work entitled *His Image, My Image*. With the help and support of the following people, I have completely rewritten the work to make it more current and relevant to today's world. I would like to thank

Waylon Ward, who so ably worked with me on the original book. His wise counsel and practical experience from the original work are not lost in this revision. I owe a debt of gratitude to my friend Waylon;

Dr. David Ferguson for his input and advice on how to make this book a more relevant work. David's Intimate Life Ministries message, which has influenced tens of thousands of people, is felt in these pages;

Ed Stewart for his expert writing skills and passionate heart, which made these words come alive to you, the reader;

Dave Bellis, my associate for twenty-one years, for coordinating this project from beginning to end. I deeply respect the value Dave brings to the finished product and the value he is to me personally;

Lynn Vanderzalm, editor with Tyndale House Publishers, for her editorial talents and insights as she reshaped and remolded many of these pages into a more concise and focused book.

PART

ONE

Who Are You?

CHAPTER 1

There's More to You
Than Meets the Eye

IMAGINE answering the doorbell and being handed a special
delivery letter. As you open it and begin to read, your eyes bug
out with excitement. You realize that this letter could change
your life and make your financial dreams come true.

The personnel office of a huge, international corporation has invited you to apply for a cushy, high-level job in which your starting
salary will be three times what you currently earn—with substantial
raises every year and staggering bonus opportunities. Surprisingly,
the qualifications are within your reach. All you have to do is
complete the enclosed application form and return it to corporate
headquarters. You sit down immediately and fill out the form.

The application states that you must submit to a thorough identity check. The personnel office requests that you send a packet of
material that describes in detail who you are.

What will you send?

You would probably start with a photograph, the most flattering
and professional pose you can find. Rummaging through a drawer,
you sort through handfuls of photos you remind yourself to burn
someday: your hideous passport photo; a swimsuit snapshot revealing those unsightly extra pounds; an old photo featuring clothes
and hairstyle that are now laughably out of date. You decide to
visit a professional photographer and do it right. You definitely
want to put your best face forward in this situation.

Next you prepare a résumé, a lengthy, detailed record of your education, career history, and civic and church activities. You may be tempted to add to the packet a list of your notable accomplishments, including offices held, honors and awards received, and promotions earned. For good measure you may slip in a few glowing letters of recommendation from friends and colleagues who know what a fine person you are. On top of the pile will be your minister's letter lauding your selfless service to God and others.

You send off your packet and sit back with a contented smile. You are confident that when the personnel people read through your application materials, the job is in the bag. But in a few days the packet is returned to you with a note from the personnel office: "Application incomplete. Your packet tells us what you look like, how well you perform, and what you have achieved, but you have not told us much about who you are."

WHO ARE YOU?

If you got that message, how would you feel? You would probably say, "But I told you who I am. What more can I tell you?"

Think about it. What makes you who you are? As suggested by the vignette above, it's not your physical attributes, your impressive education and career history, your many accomplishments, or your spiritual gifts. Furthermore, it's not your ethnic origin, family pedigree, sociopolitical persuasion, or position on the second coming of Christ. All these elements, as important as they may be to you, are not really who you are. They are merely the outer layers of your identity.

Someone has said, "Clothes make the person," but I seriously doubt that anyone takes that statement for truth. Clothes may *enhance* a person or temporarily *disguise* a person or strategically *promote* a person, but they don't *make* a person. We know that there is more to identity than how we adorn and decorate our physical bodies. All the latest diet and fitness fads promise to transform you into a new person: shed those pounds, tone up those muscles, and watch your life change. But does a transformed body affect your true identity? Of course not. You may feel better about yourself. You may live longer. But your true identity has little to do with whether you are totally fit or bulging in a few places.

So if these outer layers are only accoutrements to your true identity, who are you underneath it all? Your answer to this question will not likely qualify or disqualify you for a cushy, high-paying job. In reality, your understanding of who you are is far more important to your life than a prestigious, lucrative career.

Your core identity—and particularly your perception of it—plays a vital role in determining how you carry yourself in daily life, how much joy you experience, how you treat other people, and how you respond to God. It is essential that you know who you are apart from what you look like and what you do.

Are you happy—and sometimes even excited—about who you are and where your life is going? Do you sense inner peace even when the outer layers of your appearance, performance, and status are less than perfect? Without a clear sense of who you are beneath these many outer layers, you may experience a degree of dissatisfaction and aimlessness in life. You may feel a nagging sense of ongoing disappointment with yourself, like the university student who told me, "Josh, I know at least twenty people I'd rather be than myself." Or you may live under a dark cloud of utter despondency, such as the man who wrote me to say, "I'm alone and confused. I just don't feel that my life is worth living any more. I cry myself to sleep every night. Sometimes I just wish I were dead."

Perhaps the stark "Who are you?" question is new to you. Maybe you have been working so hard on the outer layers that you have failed to identify yourself as a person of great value and worth, made in the image of the Creator and "crowned . . . with glory and honor" (Ps. 8:5).

Many different influences have shaped how you see yourself. If you come from a behaviorist orientation, you may see life as a cosmic accident in which people are little more than programmed machines. If you share the existentialist's view, you may regard your life as an absurdity. And if you side with the humanistic evolutionists, you see yourself as only a few genetic steps removed from the ape. In any of these scenarios, the identity question is moot since the value of the human species is questionable at best. If we humans are no more than inconsequential specks in the universe, it is easy to assume that human value and significance are extremely tenuous.

Another secular view that may have influenced you states that human beings are totally independent and autonomous. Proponents of this view claim that science and technology have pushed back the barriers of more primitive days, that we are no longer bound by our ancestors' superstitions and fears. Having outgrown our need for God and religion, we are free to live any way we choose. The question of personal identity is once again pointless to those who have boldly assumed the role of Creator in human experience.

IDENTIFIED WITH THE CREATOR

A young woman commented about her friend, "She is one of the prettiest girls in the world, but she thinks she is incredibly ugly; she considers herself grotesque. That's why she can't trust anyone who says they love her. It's as if she is saying to God, 'God, if you love me, you must be a real jerk.'"

The only reality to this young woman's viewpoint is that God really does love her. Her thinking is flawed because she fails to realize that a loving God holds the key to her identity. Only he knows her true worth, which is infinitely more precious than her appearance, performance, or status. Only he can fill her longing for acceptance, love, and meaning.

People today need to know that they are loved and valued by the God who made them. This is where Christianity speaks to humanity's quest for identity and purpose in life. A personal relationship with Jesus Christ sets a person free to be all that he or she was created to be. When people respond to Christ, they don't simply embrace a philosophy of life. They establish a personal relationship with their loving Creator, the One who knows them thoroughly and loves them completely. They are eternally identified as children of the King of kings. Who could be happier and more fulfilled in life than someone with such an identity?

Sadly, the bright dawn of the third millennium finds so many people in our population—even Christians—stressed out, unhappy, unfulfilled, and even despondent. Why? Because so many of them are unsure about their true identity. Our culture largely accepts and communicates that we have little intrinsic personal value and significance. Even the church is sometimes guilty of clouding the identity issue by overstressing the old sin nature, which was crucified and buried with Christ.

Our sense of identity can be negatively affected when we hear ourselves referred to as "converted sinners." After all, we don't call a butterfly a converted caterpillar. It's a butterfly now; the old is gone, the new has come. When we trust Christ, we become new creatures. Old things pass away, and all things become new.

Through this book, I hope to help you not only understand who you really are but also thoroughly enjoy being that person. I know from personal experience that a biblical view of God, yourself, and others will be a liberating force in your life. Once you begin to identify yourself with the King, you will begin to live like a prince or princess—which is who you are. Your identity as a child of God will make a world of difference in how you view your life, your struggles, your relationships with others, and your relationship with God.

WHO YOU ARE NOT

Before we see what contributes to our true identity, we must deal with who we are not. We must dismiss our culture's prevailing myths that appearance, performance, and status form the basis of our identity as persons.

Myth #1: Image Is Everything

A pleasant and attractive physical appearance is the most highly valued personal attribute in our culture today. People are constantly asking themselves, "How do I look?" We tend to formulate our sense of value from the praise or ridicule we receive from other people based on our appearance.

It all begins in childhood. Sadly, kids can be mercilessly unkind in the way they talk about how people look. If you were called Four Eyes, Big Nose, Monkey Lip, or Lard Bottom by your peers, your sense of identity was negatively affected. Even some parents add to the cruelty. One mother jokingly referred to her daughter as "the ugly one in the family." Guess how that little girl viewed herself growing up. If you were on the receiving end of such ridicule, you likely internalized a badly distorted sense of identity: "I'm an ugly, cross-eyed nobody."

The importance we place on physical appearance is seen in the staggering amount of money we spend on clothes, cosmetics, jewelry, hairstyling, and physical fitness. For many people, merely *enhancing* physical appearance is not enough. Untold millions of dollars are spent annually to *change* physical appearance through such avenues as cosmetic surgery, liposuction, and tattoos. People today "fix" everything from noses to navels and pierce or decorate every imaginable part of the body. The closer we get to appearing "picture perfect," the greater we feel our sense of worth is to ourselves and others.

Susan is a young career woman whose job requires her to be around other attractive women daily. She is very good-looking by contemporary standards, but she does not see herself that way. Since her teenage years, Susan has been told by her mother that she is not shaped right. Instead of recognizing her value and worth as God's creation, Susan identifies herself as ugly and inadequate. She is convinced that no man will ever like her because her figure is imperfect. Working around women whom she considers beautiful only makes Susan feel worse about herself. Her insecurity over her appearance began to affect the quality of her work, and she eventually lost her job.

Sam was disfigured, the result of a childhood accident that left his face permanently scarred. As a teenager he suffered rejection from his peers, particularly the girls. His distorted sense of identity could be summarized in one word: freak. As a result, Sam withdrew socially and escaped into an unreal world, spending up to twenty hours a week watching movies. Perhaps Sam also considered the darkness of the movie theater an appropriate place for the freak he considered himself to be.

To some degree, our sense of identity has been shaped by how we appear—or think we appear—to others. We have subconsciously come to believe that beautiful people are more highly valued, and since everyone wants to be highly valued, we strive to be beautiful people.

But is our true identity determined by how we look? Of course not—it's a myth. If it were true, Jesus would never have lovingly reached out to the lepers, the poor, the crippled, and the blind—those whose physical appearance was anything but handsome or beautiful by human standards. We can be thankful that our identity as God's creation goes deeper. The Bible reminds us, "People judge by outward appearance, but the Lord looks at a person's thoughts and intentions" (1 Sam. 16:7, NLT).

I'm not saying that physical appearance is unimportant. There is nothing wrong with being well-groomed, wearing nice clothes, and otherwise taking care of your body so you look your best. The mistake is in doing so in order to *be* someone. As God's unique creation—no matter how you look—you already *are* someone of infinite value and worth.

Myth #2: You Are What You Do
Another identity myth suggests that our performance determines our worth and identity. We live in a task-oriented society that values people based on how much they do and how well they do it. And in many circles, the measure of competence is comparison. People who work harder or longer than their coworkers will likely be rewarded with the promotion. In this atmosphere we erroneously tend to connect our identity with what we do, especially as it compares to what others do. Accordingly, we may feel threatened when someone else succeeds, or we may be tempted to feel an unhealthy pride when our ability outshines another's weakness.

I know these feelings from personal experience. Years ago I was asked to speak at a singles' conference in Florida, but I was unable to attend. So I suggested that the conference director call my former roommate at Wheaton College and dear friend Dick Purnell and ask him to speak. "But we don't know Dick Purnell," the conference director complained. "Just take my word for it," I replied. "Your group will love him."

Following the conference, the director called me and jokingly said, "Are we glad you couldn't come. Dick Purnell was great!" For a few minutes there, my friend Dick loomed as a very big threat to me. The negative feelings cautioned me that I was basing my identity and security on my speaking ministry. I worked through those feelings, however, and later I was able to share the story with others, saying truthfully, "The director's comment about my not coming was one of the most profitable events in my Christian growth this year."

A few months later I was asked to speak at a conference for airline personnel. This time illness prevented me from accepting the invitation, so I again recommended Dick. Some time later I was on an airplane and met a flight attendant who had been at that conference. She said, "It was so neat that you were sick. Everyone just loved Dick!" This time my heart was immediately filled with gratefulness for Dick and his ability as a communicator.

After twice lining up Dick to speak in my place and then finding people overjoyed that I couldn't make it, I'm sure glad my identity is based on something deeper than my performance. There was a time when such responses would have threatened me and my friendship with Dick. Now I sometimes wish I had a hundred Dick Purnells to send in my place!

The person who almost surely bases his or her identity on performance is the workaholic. Many of us have a touch of this trait in our makeup. Ministers and Christian workers are often plagued by workaholism because they feel that their worth to God depends on doing the work of the ministry and fulfilling the great commission. Other workaholics feel good about themselves only when they are dog-tired from working long hours. One woman said, "I really feel good at night when I'm so tired I can hardly move."

A friend of mine tells me that he has battled this familiar pattern of equating worth and identity with performance. He was raised in a Christian home, but no matter how well he performed on a given task, his parents always wanted him to do better. He never heard them say, "Good job!" His parents' approval, especially his father's, seemed always out of reach. He told me, "At home I was always climbing a ladder without reaching the top."

Even now as an adult, my friend finds himself working to win his parents' approval. Both of them are dead now, but their standards live on within him. And because he cannot do enough to satisfy the workaholic drive within him, he is not at peace with who he is.

Do you have workaholic tendencies? They may be evident in how difficult it is for you to relax. Can you take a day off occasionally for leisure and fun? Can you sit still to read or rest without feeling anxious about tasks that need to get done? Workaholics often are depressed when their activity is hindered by the calendar (vacation, days off, weekends) or by circumstances (illness, aging, unemployment).

There is nothing wrong with putting in long hours and working hard. But if you must be active just to feel good about who you are, your identity may be based on your performance instead of your infinite worth to God apart from anything you accomplish. When Jesus selected his twelve disciples, he called them first to "be with him" and then to "send them out to preach and to have authority to drive out demons" (Mark 3:14-15). As someone once said, we were created as human *beings*, not human *doings*. No amount of activity for God can substitute for being his child.

Myth #3: You Are Somebody Only If You Have Power

A third popular identity myth is found in the question, "How important am I?" It is an issue of status. Many people do not feel good about themselves unless they have significant power, influence, or control over others. Their identity is wrapped up in the amount of status they have achieved. These people are driven to seek positions of prominence in business, politics, churches, and friendships in order to sense that their lives have value and worth.

Jack and Grace were an affable Christian couple in their early fifties. With their children grown and out of the house, Jack and Grace began to devote more time to their church as volunteers. They signed up to serve on committees, teach Sunday school, and lead Bible study groups. As an eager, energetic new member of the Christian education curriculum committee, Jack offered to serve as chairperson. Since no one else had time for the job, Jack's offer was quickly accepted. Grace got into the women's Bible study ministry and soon became a small-group leader and a member of the leadership team.

After only a brief time in their respective new roles, Jack and Grace subtly began to gather more power. Jack convinced the

committee to switch Christian education curriculum to the type
he had used as a teacher in a former church. Because the committee wanted to keep Jack, they agreed to his proposal. However, the
curriculum change wreaked havoc on the Christian education
budget and provoked a small rebellion among the teaching staff,
which was quite content with the existing materials. Jack made it
clear that he would welcome a part-time position as the Christian
education director.

In the meantime, Grace quietly assumed greater leadership of
the women's ministry. She started using her own Bible study material in her small group rather than the study material the rest of the
group was using. She also exerted her influence on the annual
women's retreat committee, pushing hard to be in charge of many
of the important details. In all her efforts, she left the impression
that her ideas and methods were superior to any others and that
the committee ought to recognize that.

After a few months, Jack and Grace's subtle grab for power in
their respective ministries began to wear thin on other volunteers.
The church leaders thanked them for their willingness to serve and
asked them to be more responsive to the gifts of others. Having
their wings of power and status abruptly clipped, Jack and Grace
eventually left the church, only to begin the process all over again
with another congregation eager for experienced volunteers.

For many people like Jack and Grace, personal worth and identity are tied at least in part to status and a sense of importance.
They are not content just to be available and serve where needed.
They must exert influence and power to feel worthwhile. If our
identity as God's children and our worth to him were based on the
level of importance and status we achieve, most of us would be out
of luck. A company can have only so many executives, a community only so many political leaders, a church only so many committee chairpersons.

The Bible is clear that our identity as God's people does not depend on the status we achieve. Contrary to the thinking that importance and status equal significance, Jesus declared, "The greatest among you must be a servant. But those who exalt themselves will be humbled, and those who humble themselves will be exalted" (Matt. 23:11-12, NLT). Christ selected twelve ordinary men as his dearest disciples and passed over the religious leaders, who were inflated with status and self-importance. He poured his heart into his disciples and entrusted them with the ministry of reaching the world with the gospel.

Whether you are regarded as somebody or nobody in your family, job, school, or church, you are somebody to God. Whether you achieve great things or small, your infinite worth and value to him are undiminished. A healthy self-identity is *seeing yourself as God sees you—no more and no less.*

A healthy self-identity is seeing yourself as God sees you—no more and no less.

BREAKING THE CHAINS FROM THE PAST

Do you see yourself described in the pages of this chapter? Are you a little discouraged to realize that you have attached so much of your worth and identity to your appearance, performance, and status? If so, you are not alone. I am convinced that most people arrive at adulthood with a skewed sense of their worth to God and to others, and as a result, they have a skewed sense of their true identity. Our parents and teachers, the media, the world of marketing and advertising, and even some of our religious experiences have reinforced the notion that our identity is shaped by how we look, how we perform, and what we achieve. Even when we understand the truth, it is difficult to break away from the ingrained thought patterns that seem to control our behavior in these areas.

We are kind of like the circus elephant whose leg is attached to a stake with a bicycle chain. How can such a flimsy chain restrict such a powerful animal? The elephant remains chained because of a memory. When the animal was very young, he tried to pull free of the chain but was not strong enough to do so. The elephant learned that the chain was stronger than he was, and he has not forgotten the lesson. Even though he is now strong enough to escape, he rarely tries because he is conditioned to captivity. The moment he *does* break away, he will be difficult to control again by any means.

Our perception of identity works in a similar manner. From childhood we are so conditioned to the importance of appearance, performance, and status that we remain bound to the false notion even when we know better. But the truth about who you are is stronger than the flimsy chains that have kept you from realizing your full potential as God's unique, valued creation. Like the elephant, you can experience freedom from those internalized bonds. You can participate fully in the joy, meaning, and fulfillment that are your inheritance as a child of God. This book will show you how.

GETTING A CLEARER PICTURE OF YOUR IDENTITY

Part of understanding who you are involves understanding who God is and experiencing his heart toward you. Reflect on the following truths about God. Take time to write your responses to the questions in a notebook or journal.

> 1. *God is love.* We read in 1 John 4:16: "God is love, and all who live in love live in God, and God lives in them" (NLT).
>   • What does it mean to you that God is love?
>   • Another part of that same verse says, "We know how

much God loves us." What does it mean to you that
the God who is love, loves *you?*

2. *God is the Creator.* We read in Isaiah 44:24: "The Lord,
your Redeemer and Creator, says: 'I am the Lord, who
made all things'" (NLT).
- What does it mean to you that God is the Creator?
- What does it mean to you that God the Creator made
you?

A second part of understanding who you are involves hearing
what God says about who *you* are. Listen to God's voice speaking
to you:

1. *God says, "You are my child."* We read in John 1:12: "But
to all who believed him and accepted him, he gave the
right to become children of God" (NLT).
- Take this verse and personalize it: "I have believed
God and accepted him. He has given me the right to
be his child."
- What does it mean to you that God cares for you
enough to make you his child, one of his very own?
- Do you sense God's heart toward you?

2. *God says, "You are chosen."* We read in Ephesians 1:4:
"For he chose us in him before the creation of the world
to be holy and blameless in his sight."
- Take this verse and personalize it: "I was chosen by
God, before he even created the world, to be holy
and blameless."
- What does it mean to you that God chose you—not
just a huge group of people, but you?
- Do you sense God's heart toward you in thinking
about you before he even created the world?

Take time to thank God for what he has revealed about himself to you. Listen to him as he speaks these words to your heart throughout the coming days and weeks. Let these truths from Scripture work their way deep into your heart and your identity.

CHAPTER 2

Solving a Case
of Mistaken Identity

D O YOU carry photos of your family in your wallet? Do you proudly display those pictures to others when you talk about your parents, your siblings, your spouse, or your children? Most people are more than eager to show off snapshots of their loved ones. But how do you feel about displaying that other picture in your wallet—your driver's license photo? Perhaps you cringe at the thought, as I do. When I pull out my wallet to brag about Dottie and our four children, I'm tempted to keep my thumb over that "mug shot." The department of motor vehicles seems skilled at taking the worst possible photos. That picture does not represent what I really look like.

Each of us carries another personal identification photo, one that is far more important than any photograph in our wallet or purse. It is a mental self-portrait, our concept of who we are. Like your driver's license photo, your inner self-portrait may or may not accurately represent the real you. Just as the quality of a photograph is diminished by lack of focus or faulty camera settings, your inner self-portrait may be inaccurate because input to your perception of who you are may be faulty or incomplete.

Take Alex, for example. The prevailing message he heard growing up was, "Alex, you can't do anything right." Was it an accurate representation of Alex? No way! Alex was inept in some areas, as we all are. But to say he cannot do *anything* right is a gross and demeaning overstatement. Yet that message was imprinted on the film of Alex's heart from childhood. Today Alex carries that distorted self-portrait wherever he goes. It is the picture of a thirty-two-year-old man who sees himself as little more than a mistake and a failure just waiting to happen. He is embarrassed to reveal his mistaken identity to others, so he is shy and antisocial.

On the other hand, consider Theresa, whose perception of her identity is suitable for framing. Theresa grew up in a home where she was cherished and nurtured by loving Christian parents. She learned early that she was God's unique and dearly loved creation. As a result, she entered adulthood very confident of her worth to God and to others. She meets new people easily, and God has used her to bring a number of her new friends to Christ.

How do you feel about your inner self-portrait? Is it more like Alex's, a picture that embarrasses you, one you would rather keep hidden? Or is it more like Theresa's, one you feel closely represents your true identity as a child of God? I speak to tens of thousands of adults and young people every year, and I visit with hundreds of them personally after the meetings. Sadly, I meet a large number of people like Alex. For example, Todd, who seemed to be very together and secure, told me, "Josh, I think of myself as a turkey. I'm so scared of what people think of me. It's hard to accept myself. I still feel afraid of looking people in the eye or even being around them. I feel like trash. My fear that people will reject me is great."

People like Alex and Todd tote around inner portraits that are badly out of focus. Precious few have the positive, nurturing background that Theresa enjoyed. Many more are struggling in life because their difficult home life, the godless culture around them, or unbiblical religious experiences—or some combination of the three—have blinded them to their true identity.

WHAT YOU SEE IS WHAT YOU GET

Whether we like it or not, our perception of who we are has a great influence on our emotional, relational, and spiritual well-being. Research has shown that we tend to act in harmony with what we perceive ourselves to be. For example, children who are ridiculed as incompetent grow up tending to make more mistakes. People who believe themselves to be unattractive often have difficulty maintaining healthy friendships. If you see yourself as a failure, you will find some way to fail no matter how hard you want to succeed. If you see yourself as adequate and capable because of your relationship with God, you will face life with greater optimism and perform nearer to your best.

As a six-year-old, Ben struggled with some early concepts in school. Witnessing his first halting efforts, Ben's parents and grandparents referred to him as dense and stupid. The more Ben heard them say it, the more he struggled with his schoolwork. As a result, one of Ben's earliest inner self-portraits had a large, one-word caption: stupid. Throughout his school years Ben subconsciously lived out the mistaken identity he had assimilated as a six-year-old.

Tanya came into her marriage to Ron without any training in homemaking. The fact that her parents did not teach her the basics about cooking left Tanya with the impression that she was incompetent in the kitchen. Ron was an old-fashioned guy who expected Tanya to have a large, delicious meal waiting for him when he arrived home, even though Tanya worked. The first several weeks of the marriage, Tanya overcooked or undercooked everything. Her lasagna came out of the oven charcoal black. Her fried chicken was raw inside. And her Jell-O was as watery as soup. Ron was less than kind. "What's wrong with you, Tanya? You can't even heat up a can of pork and beans." When Tanya pictured herself in the kitchen, she wore a big sign around her neck that said "failure." Seeing herself that way, she continued to perform miserably as a cook.

A clear perception of true identity is an invaluable asset to a healthy, happy, and productive life. But a distorted sense of identity is a hindrance to these cherished values. People like Ben and Tanya—who are convinced that they are incompetent, unlovable, ugly, or unimportant—generally don't like themselves. Struggling with self-acceptance, they project this perception on others, unable to believe anyone else could like them—even God. These negative feelings generate anxiety, stress, and depression, negatively influencing friendships, job performance, and spiritual growth.

DO YOU SEE YOURSELF WITH 20/20 VISION?

People have either a cloudy view of themselves or a clear one. Persons with a clear view of their true identity feel significant. They understand that they matter to God and to others, that the world is a better place because they are here. They are able to interact with others and appreciate their worth without feeling threatened. They radiate hope, joy, and trust because they are secure in their identity as God's children. They accept themselves as lovable, worthy, and competent members of God's creation, redeemed and reconciled to God to become all he wants them to be.

However, those with a cloudy view of their identity as God's creation display a number of debilitating traits. Let's look at three of those traits.

1. *People with a cloudy view of their identity have difficulty relating well to other people.* Absorbed with their own inadequacies, people with a faulty self-portrait lack the energy and attentiveness needed to relate positively to others. This is especially true when they are in the presence of people who remind them of their shortcomings. People with a poor sense of identity are so needy to re-

ceive attention that they are unable to give selfless attention to others. As a result, they are often regarded as uncaring or egocentric. Feelings of inadequacy from a poor sense of identity prevent them from reaching out to love and care for others.

2. *People with a poor sense of identity also look to others to determine how they view themselves at a given moment.* When they are around people who affirm and praise them, they feel worthwhile. But when family, friends, or coworkers are critical, their sense of identity takes a negative turn. They are, in effect, slaves to the opinions of others. They are not free to be themselves because their identity is dependent on the responses of others. That was the case for Bob.

Bob is a handsome, well-groomed executive type. He conveys an air of confidence that exemplifies the principles he teaches as a motivational lecturer. He speaks to business groups across the country about such topics as motivating your team, successful selling, and personal confidence. Bob's confident handshake and positive demeanor communicate success and assertiveness. So what is he doing in a counselor's office?

As Bob talks about his wife's anger, criticism, and rejection, his facade of confidence begins to crack. He is a different man at home. Conflict in his marriage erodes his sense of adequacy. Bob tearfully confesses his fear of failing without his wife's support. What happened to his unshakable confidence? In the environment of business success, his sense of worth is high. But at home, where his wife labels him a failure, his confidence is overcome by self-doubt. Without a clear picture of who he is, Bob's self-portrait will continue to change like a chameleon, based on the input he receives from those around him.

3. *People with a negative perception of their identity also struggle with negative expectations.* They walk through life expecting to be rejected, cheated, and depreciated. And since they anticipate the worst, that is what their behavior often creates for them. They en-

23

gage in self-defeating behaviors. They are distrustful and suspicious of others. They struggle between the frail hope of being acceptable to others and the underlying belief that they are unacceptable and unwanted.

Consider Karen, for example. Walking into the Christian counselor's office, she resembled a stork: tall, skinny, stoop-shouldered. Her bearing reflected her deep depression and a sense of personal inadequacy. Her dress and mannerisms conveyed that she felt anything but good about who she was. Everything Karen did communicated, "No one could ever like me."

Karen had sought out a counselor because she knew her husband, a pastor, would have to leave the ministry if her compulsive behavior came to light. She had been shoplifting for several months without getting caught. More recently, she was abusing a child she took care of. Karen's inadequate sense of identity had devalued her significantly in her own estimation. Considering herself a worthless sinner, she expected the worst from herself, opening the door for sinful actions and habits.

Happily, Karen's condition was anything but hopeless. As the counselor opened her eyes and heart to her true identity in Christ, Karen was transformed. Today, she is a different person, a loving pastor's wife and mother of three children.

ONE PERSON, MANY PORTRAITS

What do you see when you look at yourself? What do those close to you see—your parents, spouse, children, or close friends? How do you appear to those who do not know you well—the clerk at the grocery store, the neighbor on the next block, the person sitting across the aisle from you in church every Sunday? What does God see when he looks at you? The answers to these questions are vital to the process of transforming your inaccurate perception of who you are into an accurate sense of your true identity.

Obviously, everyone sees you differently from his or her own unique perspective. One way to understand the various perspectives is to consider the Johari Window, a popular tool used to explain processes of communication. Each of the four "panes" in the Johari Window represents a different perspective.

The first pane is called the *open self*, representing what you and everyone else can see about you. These are the obvious things: name, appearance, general history, surface information, anything you make public about yourself. The second pane, the *hidden self*, represents what you see but other people do not or cannot see. This is your private world of secret thoughts, ambitions, and desires.

In the first two panes, you have a good view of who you are. In the last two, your sense of identity is restricted.

The third pane, the *blind self*, represents what other people see but you do not see. For example, your spouse knows that you are a caring, patient parent, while you can see only your failures. Or your pastor sees the raw gift of teaching in the way you work with children in Sunday school, but you see yourself as inept and ineffective. Depending on how others share what they see in you, some of your blindness in this area can be removed.

Finally, the fourth pane, the *unknown self*, represents what neither you nor anyone else sees in you: forgotten experiences that have shaped your behavior, buried motives, deep hurts you have subconsciously locked away. The unknown self is the most difficult to adjust because neither you nor your loved ones can readily see it.

If you are going to alter your inner self-portrait, it is obvious you need another perspective. You need the assistance of someone who views all four panes at once, someone who sees the entire picture as it is. Furthermore, that person must be loving enough to accept you as you really are and powerful enough to help you change what you are unable to see and powerless to change.

This person, of course, is God. He is the only One who knows everything about you and loves you anyway. He is the only One who sees what you were in the past, what you are today, and what you are going to be someday. King David was in awe of how intricately and completely God knew him. He wrote:

> O Lord, you have searched me and you know me. You know when I sit and when I rise; you perceive my thoughts from afar. You discern my going out and my lying down; you are familiar with all my ways. Before a word is on my tongue you know it completely, O Lord. . . . I praise you because I am fearfully and wonderfully made; your works are wonderful, I know that full well. My frame was not hidden from you when I was made in the secret place. When I was woven together in the depths of the earth, your eyes saw my unformed body. All the days ordained for me were written in your book before one of them came to be (Ps. 139:1-4, 14-16).

No wonder David prayed with confidence about the dark, unseen areas in his life, "Search me, O God, and know my heart; test me and know my anxious thoughts. See if there is any offensive way in me, and lead me in the way everlasting" (Ps. 139:23-24).

This is our great confidence as we seek to align our self-portrait with how God sees us. God knows us completely and loves us thoroughly. Our blind self and unknown self are crystal clear to him. He knows what we need to bring those areas into the light. And he is lovingly eager to transform us into what he created us to be.

YOU CAN TRANSFORM A DEFECTIVE PORTRAIT

You may be thinking, "Josh, no wonder my life is a mess. My sense of identity is all out of whack. Is there any hope for me?" Believe me, I know exactly how you feel. If you read my biography, *A Skep-*

tic's Quest, you have an idea how my childhood with an alcoholic father left me with a very poor sense of my worth and identity as God's creation. Had I continued to allow the experiences of my childhood to color my inner self-portrait, I would be filled with rage and despair today. But as a young Christian, the inaccurate picture I inherited from the negative influences in my life began to change in the direction of my true identity.

When you align your self-portrait with God's view of you, you find a healthy identity.

I want to assure you on the basis of Scripture and from my personal experience that your imperfect inner self-portrait is not permanent. Though your self-portrait may be deeply rooted in your conscious or subconscious mind, there is hope. You can change it for an increasingly more accurate understanding of the person God made you to be. You will never see yourself as clearly as God sees you. Weaknesses and blind spots will occasionally distort your view. But you can see yourself more clearly than you do now. And the more you see yourself as God sees you—your true identity—the more you will enjoy being you. When you align your self-portrait with God's view of you, you find a healthy identity.

Bonnie, a new Christian, began attending a church where the people were highly legalistic and judgmental. They criticized her often for what they considered worldly clothing and practices. In that environment, Bonnie felt she had to prove her faith over and over again. She despaired that she would ever be worthy of God's love and salvation, something she had already received by faith. When Bonnie changed jobs and moved away from that city, the label "spiritually unworthy" was attached to her identity as a result of the negative input she had received.

The church Bonnie attended in her new location was refreshingly different. Instead of criticizing her clothing and judging her for some of her behavior, the congregation welcomed Bonnie and accepted her for who she is. In doing so, they reflected God's acceptance for Bonnie. In the new, accepting environment, Bonnie's perception of herself was transformed. She realized that she is a person of great worth to God and her loving congregation. Seeing her true identity more clearly, Bonnie experienced greater fulfillment in her walk of faith, and she became a vibrant witness of God's love.

You, too, can transform your perception from who you think you are to who you really are.

How does such a transformation take place? The chapters ahead will answer this question in much greater detail, but here is what I experienced. First, I entered into a personal, loving, dynamic relationship with God through his Son Jesus Christ. Second, I committed myself to absorb the character of God by studying his Word. Third, I allowed other Christians, particularly those who had a clearer view of my identity than I did, to help me reshape my understanding. I now see myself more as Jesus sees me—and I love what I see!

You, too, can transform your perception from who you *think* you are to who you *really* are. You can replace the distorted, embarrassing, depressing picture colored by your upbringing and experiences with a vibrant, exciting representation of the real you. I want to help you see yourself as God sees you. I want to help you discover who you really are, the special person you were created to be in God's eyes.

28

GETTING A CLEARER PICTURE OF YOUR IDENTITY

Part of understanding who you are involves understanding who God is and experiencing his heart toward you. Reflect on the following truths about God. Take time to write your responses to the questions in a notebook or journal.

1. *God is all-knowing.* We read in Psalm 139:1, 5: "O Lord, you have examined my heart and know everything about me. . . . You both precede and follow me. You place your hand of blessing on my head" (NLT).
   - What does it mean to you that God knows everything about you?
   - What does it mean to you that an all-knowing God knows that you are lovable, valuable, and competent?

2. *God is the king of the universe.* We read in 1 Chronicles 29:11: "Yours, O Lord, is the greatness, the power, the glory, the victory, and the majesty. Everything in the heavens and on earth is yours, O Lord, and this is your kingdom. We adore you as the one who is over all things" (NLT).
   - What does it mean to you that God is the king of the universe?
   - What does it mean to you that God the king rules over all the circumstances of your life?

A second part of understanding who you are involves hearing what God says about who *you* are. Listen to God's voice speaking to you:

1. *God says, "You are a masterpiece."* We read in Ephesians 2:10: "For we are God's masterpiece. He has created us anew in Christ Jesus, so that we can do the good things he planned for us long ago" (NLT).

29

- Take this verse and personalize it: "I am God's masterpiece. God made me brand-new through Christ Jesus."
- What does it mean to you that God calls you his masterpiece, a prized creation?
- Do you sense God's heart toward you as he delights in you?

2. *God says, "You are loved—eternally."* We read in Jeremiah 31:3: "I have loved you, my people, with an everlasting love. With unfailing love I have drawn you to myself" (NLT).

   - Take this verse and personalize it: "God loves me eternally, and in his love he draws me to be close to him."
   - What does it mean to you that God loves you eternally, that nothing you say or do will change his love for you?
   - Do you sense God's heart toward you in drawing you close to himself?

Take time to thank God for what he has revealed about himself to you. Listen to him as he speaks these words to your heart throughout the coming days and weeks. Let these truths from Scripture work their way deep into your heart and your identity.

CHAPTER 3

Shedding Light on Your Portrait

How do you find out who you are? You must go back to the One who made you. Your true identity is who you are in God's estimation. To gain a clear perspective of your true identity, you must see yourself as God sees you, no more and no less. The big question then is, how does God see you? Since I will talk more fully about this later in the book, I will provide only a brief answer here.

HOW DOES GOD SEE YOU?

1. *God sees you as eternally lovable.* He is your Father. He created you in his own image (see Gen. 1:26-27). You are the pinnacle of his creative genius. The psalmist marveled about God's human creation, "You made us only a little lower than God, and you crowned us with glory and honor" (Ps. 8:5, NLT). In response to your faith in Christ, the Father welcomed you into his family as his child (see John 1:12-13). God loves you so much that he appointed his angels to watch over you (see Heb. 1:14; Ps. 91:11-12). God has made provision for an ongoing, intimate relationship with you because he loves you. Nothing you can do will diminish his love for you.

2. *God sees you as infinitely valuable.* What is your value to God? At Calvary, God declared to heaven, hell, and the whole earth

that you are worth the gift of Jesus Christ, his dearly loved Son. If you ever put a price tag on yourself, it would have to read "Jesus" because that is what God paid to save you (see 1 Cor. 6:19-20; 1 Pet. 1:18-19). His death on the cross was the payment for your sins. You are "worth Jesus" to God because that is what he paid for you. This is the statement of your value to God, and God's view of who you are is true. Yet your value is a *derived* value, not a self-created value. You are of great value because that's who our loving God created you to be. You need to realize that if you had been the only person on earth, God would have sent his Son for you. To top it off, having conquered sin, death, and the grave, Jesus returned to heaven to prepare an eternal home for you (see John 14:1-3).

3. God sees you as thoroughly competent. Jesus announced to his disciples, "You will receive power when the Holy Spirit comes on you" (Acts 1:8). As a result of Christ's promise, Paul could boast, "I can do everything through him who gives me strength" (Phil. 4:13). Similarly, Paul reminded us, "Not that we are competent in ourselves to claim anything for ourselves, but our competence comes from God. He has made us competent as ministers of a new covenant" (2 Cor. 3:5-6). God gave you his power in the form of the indwelling Holy Spirit and pronounces you competent as his ambassador. Think of it: God trusts you so much that he left you on earth to complete the ministry of reconciliation Jesus began, "as though God were making his appeal through us" (see 2 Cor. 5:20). At times you may question God's judgment for placing so much confidence in you to minister in his name. You are all too aware of your weaknesses; many others seem better equipped than you. That's why Paul reminds us, "We have this treasure in jars of clay to show that this all-surpassing power is from God and not from us" (2 Cor. 4:7). Think about it: God used an amateur to build the ark, but trained professionals built the Titanic!

It is important for us to remember, however, that our lovableness, value, and competence as God's children stems from what he has made us and what he has done for us. It is not anything we are in ourselves or have done on our own that attracts God's attention or solicits his care. We owe our identity to him alone. We must continually rejoice with the psalmist, "I praise you because I am fearfully and wonderfully made; your works are wonderful, I know that full well" (Ps. 139:14).

LIVING IN THE LIGHT

So why do so many us live as if we do not believe that God finds us lovable, valuable, and competent? The apostle Paul describes our condition: "For you were once darkness, but now you are light in the Lord" (Eph. 5:8). Before we became believers, we lived in darkness. But when we surrendered our lives to Christ's lordship, it's as if he turned on the light so that we can see the truth.

God's portrait of you reveals that he sees you as lovable, valued, and competent.

Have you ever been in an art gallery when the room lights are on but the spotlights that shine on various portraits are not? With the room lights on, you can see the portrait frames, and you may even be able to make out some of the features in the portraits. But when the spotlights are turned on, when an intense light is directed on each portrait, you can see all of the details of the portrait—the facial expression, the skin tone, the eye color, the curve of the lips. When the spotlights are on, you can see the person as the artist intended you to see him or her.

That's what God's light is like for us. It shines brightly on us and shows us who he created us to be.

But many of us have not seen God's portrait of us very clearly. The light of his truth concerning our true identity has been blocked or limited by a number of circumstances in our lives. When God's light is blocked, our vision concerning who we are is hampered, and our lives suffer accordingly. Consider first how God provided for the light to come into our lives. Scripture identifies three sources of God's light in the world:

1. *Jesus Christ is the primary source of the light.* John announced about Jesus, "Life itself was in him, and this life gives light to everyone" (John 1:4, NLT). Jesus said of himself, "I am the light of the world. Whoever follows me will never walk in darkness, but will have the light of life" (John 8:12). The way we come into the light is to come into a personal relationship with Christ. We grow in the knowledge that we are loved, valued, and made competent as this relationship grows deeper through intimate fellowship with Christ.

2. *God's Word, the Bible, is another source of the light.* King David wrote, "Your word is a lamp to my feet and a light for my path" (Ps. 119:105). The more we open our minds and hearts to the Word of God, the more light we enjoy. In the light of God's Word we see that God loves us, values us, and makes us competent. Believers who do not study and experience Scripture in daily life lack the light they need.

3. *Other believers are a source of God's light.* The One who proclaimed, "I am the light of the world," also told his followers, "You are the light of the world" (Matt. 5:14). Being in relationship with Christ, the Light, fills us with light. As we share the light of Christ and his Word with one another, we grow in our understanding that God loves us, values us, and makes us competent. This is a primary reason why we are instructed, "Let us not give up meeting together, as some are in the habit of doing, but let us encourage one another—and all the more as you see the Day approaching" (Heb. 10:25). We need interaction with other believers in order to flood our lives with God's light, which reveals our true identity.

WHERE WERE YOU EXPOSED TO THE LIGHT?

Several critical questions will help you discover why you sometimes live as if you don't know who you are as God's beloved, valued, and competent child. Ask yourself these questions:

How Much Light Was in Your Home When You Were a Child?
Were your parents and other significant adults in your life believers? If so, did they model a loving relationship with Jesus Christ, or was their "religion" one of rules, prohibitions, and guilt? If the latter is true, you did not get a true picture of how God sees you. You may have grown up seeing God as a demanding ogre who was ready to slap you down the moment you stepped out of line. You may have grown up thinking that God's love was something you had to earn. You may have perceived that your value was based on your performance, not on your intrinsic value to God.

How much of the light of God's Word did you see in your home? Did your parents, grandparents, and other significant relatives read and revere the Bible? Were the Bible and other Bible-related materials read to you as a child? Did your family have devotions in which the Bible was explored and discussed in ways that were appropriate to your level of understanding? Were biblical stories and concepts discussed informally in your home? If you grew up surrounded by positive interaction and application of Scripture, a significant amount of light was shed in your life. But if the Bible was missing in the lives of your relatives and in your upbringing, the resulting darkness may have contributed to your confusion about who you are in Christ today.

Did you attend church as a child and teenager? Was the truth of the Scriptures taught and modeled in the life of your church? Did your family encourage your participation in events that brought you together with other Christians your age, such as Sunday school, vacation Bible school, Bible clubs, or youth group meetings and activities? As you were able to gather with other Christians for fellowship and study, you were exposed to more of God's light. If church and other Christian group activities were not part of your upbringing, your sense of identity may be limited by the lack of light.

How Much Light Was in the Culture around You?
I believe that society has moved from the post-Christian era, as the late Dr. Francis Schaeffer called the 1970s and 1980s, to the anti-Christian era. A generation ago, Christians were simply ignored. "Do your religious thing if it works for you," the world said, "but don't expect us to go along." Today the world is more hostile toward us and the values we understand from Scripture to be absolutes. "How dare you try to impose your values on society," we hear now. "Choosing what is right and wrong is a personal decision, not society's decision or the church's decision."

If your environment was strongly influenced by apathy and/or antagonism toward God, the Bible, and Christianity, then the light was blocked from your life by the deep shadows of the anti-Christian culture. Instead of portraying humanity as loved, valued, and made competent by God, our culture has turned the spotlight on human goodness and achievement. As a result of this darkened approach to who we are, you received little positive input from your environment concerning your true identity.

How does the culture shut out the light? One of the primary ways culture blinds people to the truth is via the media. The prevailing messages of our culture—God is a crutch for the weak; Jesus Christ was no more than a good moral teacher; the Bible is fallible and uninspired; moral absolutes are obsolete—live in our homes like pets. They flow in through the television programs we watch and the Internet sites we visit.

How Much Light Came through Your Peers?
What kind of people did you hang out with when you were a child and teenager? What did your friends, your college roommates, and

other members of your peer group believe about Jesus Christ, the Bible, and Christians?

In a national study of Christian young people, we asked over 3,700 young people who attended church to prioritize what they desired for their future. From a list of fifteen desirable conditions, their top three were (1) "having one marriage partner for life"; (2) "good physical health"; (3) "having close, personal friendships."[1] The view we have of ourselves is so often influenced by our peers because we all want and need close, personal friendships.

Peer pressure, for example, is sometimes misunderstood. Some think that the temptation for a person to drink or take drugs originates from the desire for alcohol or drugs, and that peers are simply the ones who are the vehicle of that temptation. But the allurement to an unacceptable activity or behavior in many cases is not the thing that tempts us; rather, it is the inner desire to be *accepted* by peers. What we want our peers to think of us is a powerful motivating force in each of us. And to the extent that your childhood peers were in darkness about God's view of identity, they likely blocked the light from your understanding.

God's portrait of you reveals that he sees you as lovable, valued, and competent. If you are unable to see that portrait clearly, it may be because the spotlight of God's truth has been blocked or dimmed. When you allow the light of the person of Jesus Christ, the Bible, and other Christians to shine on your portrait, you will begin to see yourself as God created you.

GETTING A CLEARER PICTURE OF YOUR IDENTITY
Part of understanding who you are involves understanding who God is and experiencing his heart toward you. Reflect on the fol-

[1]Josh McDowell and Bob Hostetler, *Right From Wrong* (Nashville: Word, 1994), 261.

lowing truths about God. Take time to write your responses to the questions in a notebook or journal.

1. *God is light.* We read in 1 John 1:5: "God is light; in him there is no darkness at all."
   - What does it mean to you that God is light?
   - What does it mean to you that God has made you to be light (Eph. 5:8)?

2. *God is kind.* We read in Psalm 145:8: "The Lord is kind and merciful" (NLT).
   - What does it mean to you that God is kind?
   - What does it mean to you that this kind God has chosen *you* to be his child?

A second part of understanding who you are involves hearing what God says about who *you* are. Listen to God's voice speaking to you:

1. *God says, "You are the light of the world."* We read in Matthew 5:14: "You are the light of the world—like a city on a mountain, glowing in the night for all to see." (NLT).
   - Take this verse and personalize it: "I am one of God's lights to the world."
   - What does it mean to you that God trusts you to be his light for everyone to see?
   - Do you sense God's heart toward you in valuing you enough to make you one of his representatives in the world?

2. *God says, "You are a child of the light."* We read in 1 Thessalonians 5:5: "You are all children of the light and of the day; we don't belong to darkness and night" (NLT).

38

- Take this verse and personalize it: "God has made me a child of the day. I don't need to live in darkness anymore."
- What does it mean to you that God has made you a child of the light?
- Do you sense God's heart toward you in flooding your life with light because he is light?

Take time to thank God for what he has revealed about himself to you. Listen to him as he speaks these words to your heart throughout the coming days and weeks. Let these truths from Scripture work their way deep into your heart and your identity.

CHAPTER 4

How Unmet Needs Affect Your Identity

I f the three sources of light—Jesus, the Bible, and other Christians—are blocked in your life, you may live with many unmet needs. Until these needs are healed, they can distort your sense of identity. Joanna's experience is a good example.

Joanna, an attractive Christian woman, summarized herself this way: "A worm doesn't adequately describe how I feel about myself. A worm can crawl underground and hide without leaving a trail. I'm more like the ugly slugs on my patio. Everywhere they go, they leave this horrible trail behind them. That's what I'm like; I mess up everything wherever I go." What a sad description for the life of a believer!

Joanna is in the dark concerning her true identity. She is not a worm or a slug. She makes mistakes just as we all do, but she certainly does not "mess up everything" wherever she goes.

Joanna has many unmet needs in her life, and as a result she has a distorted sense of her true identity. This faulty identity has imprisoned her in depression, self-condemnation, and despair, virtually nullifying her Christian growth and witness.

When a believer's true identity as God's beloved, valued, competent child is obscured due to a lack of light, the results are pathetic. Generally speaking, such persons tend toward a fearful, pessimistic view of the world and their ability to cope with its challenges. They regard new or unexpected situations as threats to their happiness and security. They sense that the world is closing in on them, suffocating them, crushing them. All their difficulties seem to stem from personal failure.

People who are confused about their identity tend to endure what life deals them without challenging it or attempting to change it. They see themselves as victims in a hostile environment.

By contrast, persons who walk in the light of being loved, valued, and equipped by God regard the world as a challenge to be faced, an opportunity to exercise their trust in Christ. They accept that, by the grace and power of God in their lives, they can change their environment for the better. They know that their destiny lies in what God can do through them, that they can and will accomplish significant things for eternity even in difficult circumstances.

A skewed sense of identity also affects relationships. Living on the defensive, people with a faulty sense of identity interpret other people's messages and motives from the inaccurate self-portrait they carry. For example, Joanna has difficulty accepting praise or compliments from others. In her opinion, a slug cannot possibly be pretty or helpful or generous. She further reasons, "Can anyone with such mistaken perceptions of me be trustworthy?" Until her inner self-portrait is transformed, Joanna will be skeptical of even the most sincere and well-meaning attempts to build her up.

LIVING IN THE SHADOW OF UNMET NEEDS

How do people like Joanna arrive at such an inaccurate view of who they are? I believe it relates directly to the amount of God's light that filters into their lives. When people are encouraged toward an intimate, ongoing relationship with Christ, his Word, and his people, the light of God's truth floods in. And when this happens, people's spiritual, emotional, and relational needs are met, and people gain a clearer perspective of their true identity as God's beloved, valued, competent children.

Sadly, however, Joanna and many hurting people like her live with gaping needs that cast a shadow on the light and distort their ability to see themselves as God sees them. As those needs are met through Jesus, his Word, and other Christians, these needy people will come to see their true identity.

Our Most Significant Needs
What are those unmet needs that can cast a shadow on our self-portraits? While we could list many of them, let's look at a list of our top ten emotional needs. This list comes from the research and work of David Ferguson, who directs Intimate Life Ministries in Austin, Texas. David and his wife, Teresa, have helped thousands of believers discover their true identity as children of God (see the appendix for more information about their ministry).

In his book *The Great Commandment Principle*, David Ferguson identifies from Scripture ten essential human needs that must be met in order for us to experience intimacy in our relationship with God and others.[2] When these needs go unmet, people feel alone and their sense of true identity is diminished. We all need

1. Attention
2. Acceptance
3. Appreciation
4. Support
5. Encouragement
6. Affection
7. Respect
8. Security
9. Comfort
10. Approval

[2]The list and explanation are adapted from David Ferguson's *The Great Commandment Principle* (Wheaton, Ill.: Tyndale House Publishers, 1998), 44-52.

In an attempt to help you understand what your primary needs are from this list of ten needs, let's look at each need more closely.

1. *Attention.* Our need for attention means that we need people to think about us and convey appropriate care, interest, concern, and support for us. When we give each other attention, we are experiencing God's Word as expressed in 1 Corinthians 12:25: "This makes for harmony among the members, so that all the members care for each other equally" (NLT). Attention says, "I will enter your world and get to know your world because I care for you."

2. *Acceptance.* Our need for acceptance means that we need people to receive us willingly, to regard us as good and proper, even if they disagree with us. When we accept each other, we are following the biblical mandate expressed in Romans 15:7: "So accept each other just as Christ has accepted you; then God will be glorified" (NLT). Acceptance says, "Even if nothing about you changed, I would love you anyway, just the way you are."

3. *Appreciation.* Our need for appreciation means that we need people not only to recognize who we are and what we have done but also to communicate to us with words and feelings that they are grateful. When we appreciate each other, we are following the biblical pattern expressed in 1 Corinthians 11:2: "I praise you for remembering me in everything." Appreciation says, "Thank you for your thoughtfulness. I am so grateful that you called."

4. *Support.* Our need for support means that we need people to come alongside us and gently help us carry a problem or struggle. When we support each other, we are experiencing Galatians 6:2: "Carry each other's burdens, and in this way you will fulfill the law of Christ." Support says, "I sense you can use some help. Please allow me to help you carry some of the load."

5. *Encouragement.* Our need for encouragement means that we need people not only to urge us forward but also to inspire us with courage, spirit, or hope. When we encourage each other, we are following the biblical mandate expressed in 1 Thessalonians 5:11:

"Encourage each other and build each other up, just as you are already doing" (NLT). Encouragement says, "So many people are going to be positively affected by your good work on this project. I know you will finish it successfully."

6. *Affection.* Our need for affection means that we need people to communicate care and closeness through physical touch and affirming words. When we show each other affection, we are experiencing Romans 16:16: "Greet one another with a holy kiss." Affection puts a hand on someone's shoulder and says, "I'm so glad you're here today."

7. *Respect.* Our need for respect means that we need people to value us, to recognize our worth, and to esteem us. When we respect each other, we are living out 1 Peter 2:17: "Show respect for everyone. Love your Christian brothers and sisters. Fear God. Show respect for the king" (NLT). Respect says, "I need your input on this because your insights are so valuable to me."

8. *Security.* Our need for security means that we need people to protect us from danger, deprivation, and harmful relationships. When we give each other security, we are following the biblical desire expressed in Psalm 122:6-8: "'May those who love you be secure. May there be peace within your walls and security within your citadels. . . . Peace be within you.'" Security says, "I am committed to you, and as God allows and provides, I will meet your needs both now and in the future."

9. *Comfort.* Our need for comfort means that we need people not only to ease our grief or pain but also to give us strength and hope to go on. When we comfort each other, we are experiencing 2 Corinthians 1:3-4: "Praise be to the God and Father of our Lord Jesus Christ, the Father of compassion and the God of all comfort, who comforts us in all our troubles, so that we can comfort those in any trouble with the comfort we ourselves have received from God." Comfort says, "I am so sorry to hear about your daughter's divorce. How hard that must be for you. Know that I will pray for

you and be available to listen to you and go through this with you during the coming months."

10. *Approval.* Our need for approval means that we need people to express a favorable opinion about us and to affirm us as satisfactory. When we give each other approval, we are following the biblical pattern expressed in Romans 14:18: "If you serve Christ with this attitude, you will please God. And other people will approve of you, too" (NLT). Approval says, "I am pleased with you."

Not only has God created us with these needs, but he also wants to meet those needs in us. He has chosen to meet those needs not only through himself but also through other people. After God made the first human, Adam, and placed him in the perfection of the Garden of Eden, the Creator declared, "It is not good for the man to be alone. I will make a helper suitable for him" (Gen. 2:18). We see that God desires to involve others with him in removing this aloneness. His plan includes meeting our innate aloneness needs through his direct intervention and through others such as a spouse, other family members, and the church.

But when our vital needs are not met, God's light is blocked and our true identity is hidden in the shadows. Consider the consequences when each of the three sources of light is obscured.

In the Dark about Being Loved by God

Kendall attends a large Bible study group for singles nearly every week, but most people around him don't even know he is there. He arrives barely on time, sits by himself, and heads for the door right after the closing prayer. Whenever someone tries to engage him in conversation, Kendall looks uncomfortable and offers little information about himself.

Alvin, one of the group leaders, noticed Kendall and decided to befriend him. For several weeks Alvin sought out Kendall after Bible study just to say hello. Eventually Alvin convinced Kendall to meet him for lunch. After a couple of meetings over lunch and breakfast, Kendall began to open up to his persistent new friend Alvin.

"No way can God love me," Kendall said one day. "He just puts up with me because I have accepted Christ as my Savior. He forgives my sins because I confess them according to 1 John 1:9, so he has to forgive me. But God will never love me as his child. I know what I have done. Maybe in heaven it will be different. But for now, I'm just lucky to be saved."

Alvin wisely did not respond to Kendall's confession by ramming Scripture verses about God's love down his throat. Instead he probed gently about Kendall's background. He learned that Kendall grew up in a non-Christian home. His father's business kept him away from home for weeks at a time. When Dad returned, Mom pulled out a list of Kendall's misdeeds during the trip. Dad meted out a whipping appropriate to the crimes and warned the boy to be-

---

Their sense of belonging is diminished when they do not sense love from God or others.

---

have during his next trip. Kendall did not recall that his father ever touched him affectionately or said, "I love you."

How do people like Kendall fail to see themselves as the objects of God's unconditional love? Their sense of belonging is diminished when they do not sense love from God or others. Since they are not loved by the people from whom they most need love, they can logically assume that they are unlovable. They not only project this perception on others around them and on God, but they can also subconsciously behave in ways that communicate, "Don't get too close because I'm not worth loving."

It is difficult to believe that God can love us if our specific needs for love have gone unmet.

1. Affection. People may feel unloved when their need for *affection* goes unmet. Like Kendall, many men and women grew up missing appropriate hugs, kisses, pats, and caresses from parents, particularly from their fathers. When the God-ordained need for affection is not properly met, people may set about to meet that need in whatever way they can, often resulting in inappropriate and potentially harmful behavior.

One response is to keep God and others at a safe distance. This was Kendall's response, which is what made Alvin's attempts at friendship so difficult. As long as Kendall remained aloof, he was not reminded of his unlovableness. But by remaining aloof, Kendall was unable to exercise his spiritual gifts and minister to the needs of others around him, rendering him an ineffective member of the body of Christ. Because he found it very difficult to express affection, he passed on a lack of love to others.

Other symptoms of a lack of affection appear as the opposite of withdrawal. Some people become clingy in their relationships, jealously demanding time and affection from friends or family members. Others may seek affection through promiscuous sexual relationships or through pornography and self-gratification. After several months of meeting with Alvin, Kendall confided that his hunger for affection had spawned an addiction to pornography and masturbation.

2. Acceptance. People may feel unloved when their need for *acceptance* goes unmet. Kendall grew up sensing that his dad was interested only in the boy he *could be* if he behaved better, not in the boy he *was.* People who do not feel accepted tend to strive to be someone or something else instead of relaxing and enjoying who they are. Why? Because they perceive that nobody loves them for who they are. They may also struggle with feeling acceptable to God, so they try to earn his acceptance through their religious efforts.

3. *Approval.* People may feel unloved when their need for *approval* goes unmet. Before Jesus had preached one sermon or performed one miracle, God the Father announced, "You are my Son, whom I love; with you I am well pleased" (Mark 1:11). We all need to know that someone lovingly approves of us apart from what we accomplish or contribute. Children need to sense their parents' approval—whether or not they earn straight A's, score a soccer goal, or hit a home run in Little League. Kendall received attention from his father only when he did something wrong. This lack of approval left Kendall feeling unloved.

People who sense disapproval are more likely to become a doormat to others. They will do anything for anybody in order to gain a measure of approval. Many teenage girls yield to a boy's sexual advances because it is one way to gain the approval they missed from their parents. The unmet need for approval drives some believers to rigid and legalistic behavior. They become convinced that they must attend every service, pray longer or louder, give more to missions, and accept more responsibilities at church to gain the approval they seek.

4. *Respect.* People may feel unloved when their need for *respect* goes unmet. We all need to feel important, to feel that our personality, our gifts, and our contributions are needed. Kendall grew up feeling that his only role in life was to give his father an excuse to vent his anger.

A chief symptom indicating that our need for respect has gone unmet is a lack of self-respect. When we think that others consider us unimportant, we see ourselves as unimportant. Low self-esteem is evidenced by inattention to appearance, grooming, and habits of health. A sense of personal unimportance can lead to lack of respect for the law, the commands of Scripture, other people, and the dignity of human life, even one's own.

Alvin met with Kendall patiently and persistently for a few months. Eventually the leader convinced Kendall to join one of the care groups in the singles' ministry. In the group Kendall became the object of the loving concern of eight other single men and women. As his long-ignored needs for affection, acceptance, approval, and respect were met through his new friends, Kendall's perception of his identity was transformed. He had *heard* about God's love from Scripture since he was a boy. As he began to *experience* it through the care of his friends, the growing intensity of God's light in his soul revealed his lovableness to God. Within two years Kendall was a member of the leadership team, lovingly seeking out others as Alvin had ministered to him.

IN THE DARK ABOUT BEING VALUED BY GOD

Katrina was destined to be a model and an actress before she was born. When Katrina was six months old, Joyce, her unmarried mother, moved them to Los Angeles and enrolled her daughter with a modeling agency to do commercials for baby products. The little girl's childhood was tightly scheduled with modeling classes and competitions, dancing and acting classes, and auditions for commercials and bit parts in television shows. Joyce personally supervised a strict diet and fitness regimen to make sure Katrina glowed with health and vitality. She was determined to keep her daughter on the fast track to Hollywood stardom.

The night Katrina graduated from a posh L.A. prep school, she disappeared. She said good-bye to her mother after the ceremony, supposedly on her way to a country club for the senior class all-night celebration. Katrina never came home the next morning. Months later she was found in a shelter for homeless teens in Baltimore, dirty and scarred from street life.

Joyce paid for Katrina to be flown home. "Look at your hair, your skin," Joyce cried at their reunion. "You have ruined your life."

"No, Mother," Katrina returned angrily. "I have ruined *your* life. I never had a life, not until I left home. You robbed me of my childhood. You turned me into a real-life Barbie doll for your own amusement. I was your daughter only when I was posing or performing. Well, your Barbie doll has grown up now, Mother, and you can't play with me anymore."

Katrina stayed in Los Angeles and got a job waiting tables. At the invitation of a former classmate, she began attending a small church. Even though the members of the church did not know about Katrina's past, she had difficulty at first accepting their warm hospitality. She had the same misgivings about God, thinking he would not want someone who had done what she had done. Her value as a person had been attached to her appearance and performance for too long.

Many people come into adulthood with a clouded sense of their worth to God and others. Children are often valued by their parents and other significant adults on the basis of their achievements instead of their innate worth as individuals for whom God paid the supreme price of his Son. And these children carry their inaccurate self-portraits into adulthood, feeling they gain God's attention only by their activity. When specific needs go unmet, people who believe they are unworthy become mired in defeating behaviors.

1. *Attention.* People often feel unworthy when their need for *attention* goes unmet. We give attention to others by entering into their world, showing interest in the things that interest them. A young child gains attention when Mom or Dad gets down on the floor and plays what the child wants to play. By forcing Katrina into her own world of modeling and performing, Joyce failed to meet Katrina's need for attention. Katrina's only value to her mother came from her success in competitions and modeling jobs.

People who are starved for attention sometimes lack confidence in their social skills. They are under such pressure to perform that they cannot enjoy relationships. Friends, coworkers, and even strangers are viewed as competition for the attention of others. Needing others around them to assure their value by comparison, these people are often uncomfortable and fearful being alone.

2. *Security*. People may feel unworthy when their need for *security* goes unmet. Insecure people often depend on a stockpile of material possessions for security. They need a significant amount of structure and external control in their lives to feel safe. Even so, they tend to be pessimistic about the future, expecting the worst to happen.

3. *Comfort*. People often feel unworthy when their need for *comfort* goes unmet. When we get hurt emotionally or relationally, God's prescription for healing includes the loving comfort of others (see Matt. 5:4; 2 Cor. 1:3-4). Those who suffer life's deep hurts alone sense that they must not be worth much to the people who ignore their pain and need for comfort. As a result, hurting people often erect barriers between themselves and others to prevent further hurt. Even family members and friends are sometimes regarded as threats to their peace. The end result is relationships that are strained instead of nurturing.

Katrina continues to struggle with her sense of worth to God and others. But her relationship with a few caring young women at church continues to grow. They show interest in Katrina for who she is, not for who she was or for what she accomplished. She has told two of the young women about the pain in her relationship with her mother. They tearfully comforted her. Katrina is beginning to feel valued as a person for the first time in her life. Her new friends expect that Katrina will open her heart to Christ soon.

IN THE DARK ABOUT OUR COMPETENCE TO GOD

When you understand Joanna's background, it is no surprise that she felt like a slug who messes up everything wherever she goes. Joanna's stepfather, Buck, was a hardworking provider for his daughter and her mother. Joanna hardly remembered her real father, who died when she was two. But Buck was a demanding perfectionist who pushed Joanna to be the best at everything she tried. His prime method of motivation was humiliation. If she did not make an all-out effort, Buck was on her case. His pet names for her were Dummy, Slowpoke, Clumsy, Tubby, and Numbhead. The more he ragged on Joanna, the more frazzled she became and the more mistakes she made.

Joanna entered adulthood with the I-can't-do-anything-right attitude burned into her subconscious. Flustered under pressure to succeed, she failed to keep her first two jobs. She has managed to keep a low-stress, low-pay job for ten years, but her performance record is less than sterling.

The cloud of incompetence hovering over Joanna is largely the result of crying needs that have gone unmet.

1. *Encouragement*. People may feel incompetent when their need for *encouragement* goes unmet. An environment of criticism, blame, and humiliation injures the spirit, shakes confidence, and crushes motivation. People who feel incompetent may sometimes become defensive in their behavior and conversation. "I knew it wouldn't work; nothing I do ever works," they lament. "Why should I even try when everything I touch turns to dust?" People who are not encouraged develop a pessimistic outlook on life.

2. *Support*. People may feel incompetent when their need for *support* goes unmet. Everyone needs a burden-bearer, someone who will come alongside and share the weight of a difficult task or trial. Instead of providing needed support, Buck left Joanna to fend for herself in her efforts. Unable to live up to her stepfather's demanding standards, Joanna battled feelings of hopelessness that further hindered her attempts at success.

3. *Appreciation*. People may feel incompetent when their need for *appreciation* goes unmet. No one is 100 percent competent. Some

people struggle to complete tasks with only a small degree of success. But everyone can be appreciated for something, for things such as effort, helpfulness, a positive attitude, persistence in adversity, or a willingness to try. Unappreciated people like Joanna find that even their successes are insufficient to erase the labels they have adopted for themselves, such as a slug who messes things up wherever she goes.

As you read through the ten needs in this chapter, did a few of them stand out to you? Could you identify needs that have gone unmet during your childhood and youth? Could you also identify with some of the resulting symptoms of unmet needs that may have been hindering your perception of your true identity as God's beloved, valued, competent child?

Someone has said that a problem defined is half solved. You may now be aware of some areas where God's light concerning your identity is needed. This is an important step in the direction of transforming your inner self-portrait. In the chapters ahead we will tackle the question of how to move toward that transformation. Before we do, it is important for you to understand a few more factors that played a role in how you arrived at your present, inaccurate picture of who you are.

GETTING A CLEARER PICTURE OF YOUR IDENTITY

Part of understanding who you are involves understanding who God is and experiencing his heart toward you. Reflect on the following truths about God. Take time to write your responses to the questions in a notebook or journal.

> 1. *God is compassionate.* We read in Psalm 86:15: "But you, O Lord, are a compassionate and gracious God, slow to anger, abounding in love and faithfulness."
> • What does it mean to you that God is compassionate?
> • How has God's compassion touched your life?

2. *God is faithful.* We read in Hosea 2:20: "I will be faithful to you and make you mine, and you will finally know me as Lord" (NLT).
   - What does it mean to you that God is faithful to you?
   - What does it mean to you that this faithful God has made you his?

A second part of understanding who you are involves hearing what God says about who *you* are. Listen to God's voice speaking to you:

1. *God says, "You are secure."* We read in Philippians 4:19: "This same God who takes care of me will supply all your needs from his glorious riches, which have been given to us in Christ Jesus" (NLT).
   - Take this verse and personalize it: "I can be secure because God has promised to supply all my needs."
   - What does it mean to you that God will supply all your needs?
   - Do you sense God's heart toward you in making all of his glorious riches available to you in order to meet your needs?

2. *God says, "You are understood."* We read in Luke 12:30-31: "Your Father already knows your needs. He will give you all you need from day to day if you make the Kingdom of God your primary concern" (NLT).
   - Take this verse and personalize it: "God, my Father, knows all of my needs. If I choose to place him first in my life, he will give me everything I need."
   - What does it mean to you that God not only knows your needs but also will meet those needs?
   - Do you sense God's heart toward you in making sure your needs are met?

Take time to thank God for what he has revealed about himself to you. Listen to him as he speaks these words to your heart throughout the coming days and weeks. Let these truths from Scripture work their way deep into your heart and your identity.

PART

TWO

Who Told You Who You Are?

CHAPTER 5

The Influence of Your Family

Where did your inner self-portrait come from? In reality, it did not begin as a self-portrait at all. You inherited your initial perception of your identity from other sources. Beginning with your birth through childhood and early youth, other people impressed on you certain elements of identity by the way they treated you and talked to you. If you were cherished and coddled like a prince or princess, you likely grew up thinking you were royalty. If you were constantly berated for your incompetence, you may have pictured yourself as a slug who messes up everything. In your childish innocence and naïvete, you accepted the portrait that was handed to you.

But was that portrait accurate? Not entirely, and for many of us it was not even close. You are an imperfect person who was raised by imperfect people. To the degree that God's light penetrated your environment and shaped your life through the people around you, your inner portrait was accurate. If the sources of your earliest portrait affirmed that you were created in God's image and are worth the death of his Son, you were blessed to grow up with a good likeness. But if your environment lacked an abundance of God's light concerning your true identity, you may have grown up with a distorted sense of identity, as did Kendall, Katrina, and Joanna in the previous chapter.

Only when you become a mature young person or adult are you able to determine if the picture you inherited accurately represents how God sees you. And only as you clearly see the portrait you inherited and understand how it came about are you able to pursue transformation of that perception.

Four general sources of input shaped your perception of identity during childhood:

1. Your family, including parents, stepparents, older siblings, grandparents, and other close relatives
2. Significant non-related adults and peers, such as teachers, coaches, close friends, and schoolmates
3. The culture in which you grew up
4. Your religious education and experiences as a child and youth

If the sources of your earliest portrait affirmed that you were created in God's image and are worth the death of his Son, you were blessed to grow up with a good likeness.

In order to evaluate the impact of each of these sources on your earliest perceptions of identity, you must ask this question: "How did light filter through each source as my sense of identity was being shaped?" We will talk about the first source—family—in this chapter and the remaining three sources in the next chapter.

YOUR PARENTS: FROM THE IDEAL TO THE REAL

What is God's ideal plan for developing a healthy sense of identity in children? It does not happen by accident. God's optimum design begins with a Christian family—a man and a woman who are fully committed to love God and one another as husband and wife. This couple then becomes the primary conduit of God's light to illuminate the true identity of their children. In the early years of the children's development, they observe their parents' godly example, receive their loving care, and absorb biblical instruction. All of this allows the children to see themselves as God sees them. In this environment, it is quite natural for children to trust Christ personally and begin to live out their identity as children of God.

This scenario, of course, is the ideal. My family setting was far from this ideal, and perhaps yours was too. You may have grown up in a single-parent family or a blended family of a parent and stepparent. You may have been raised by grandparents, older siblings, or other relatives or guardians. Perhaps the adults who raised you were not Christians; maybe they were even cruel and abusive to you. Even if they were believers, they may have misunderstood or ignored the importance of their role in shaping your sense of identity.

Because you did not choose your parents or guardians, you are not responsible for how your family influenced your sense of identity. But you must realize that in your upbringing, every degree of variation from God's ideal design has affected how you interpret your identity today.

HOW YOUR PARENTS SHAPED YOUR SELF-PORTRAIT

No matter who served as your parent figures, their evaluation of who you are was transferred to your impressionable mind as a young child. You saw yourself in the light of their prevailing attitudes and actions toward you. The relational atmosphere in your family contributed more to your initial sense of identity than did any other influence. Understanding that atmosphere is a key ingredient in transforming your perception to how God sees you.

Consistent, daily parental attitudes and input seem to be more influential in shaping a child's identity than any specific events. Those seemingly small but repeated experiences, though you may not remember them, provided much of the color to your first inner portrait.

A young couple I know had just moved into a new house, and they were up to their elbows in landscaping. Having set out twenty young azalea bushes as well as other shrubs around the yard, the wife began the process of planting them. For several days their three-year-old daughter played in the yard alone while her mother diligently prepared the soil, dug the holes, and set the plants in the ground. The three-year-old repeatedly begged for her mommy to play with her. "I have to get these bushes planted," the mother replied impatiently. "We can play later."

One morning the bored little girl watched longingly as her mother poured all her energy into the care of each delicate azalea bush. She had been warned not to bug her mother about playing with her. But the neglected three-year-old could no longer suppress the question that had formed in her innocent thoughts: "Mommy, do you love me as much as you love your flowers?"

From her mother's preoccupation with landscaping, this little girl was receiving a message about herself: "I am not as lovable as Mommy's flowers." Perhaps there were other subtle ways in which this mother allowed the activities of daily life to push her daughter's need for attention to the back burner. This woman would vehemently disagree that she loved caring for her prized azaleas or singing in the choir or watching her favorite television shows more than she loved her daughter. But every time she unwittingly elevated another activity over the little girl's needs, that child's impressionable mind received input concerning her worth to her mother.

Young children have no clear picture of who they are apart from the input they receive. They see themselves primarily through the eyes of their parents or guardians. Children who hear from a parent that they are bad or lazy or dumb will accept that evaluation and tend to live it out.

Larry has battled deep-seated depression and lack of self-confidence ever since he can remember. At age twenty-six, he still has not decided what to do with his life. He feels frustrated, insecure, and very inadequate in most situations. When Larry was a boy, his father repeatedly called him Stupid. Even today Larry's dad tells him that he can't do anything right. Larry has been living out his father's portrait of an inept, incompetent son for twenty-six years. His perception of who he is must be transformed to match how his heavenly Father sees him.

Children who are loved and valued by their parents will grow to live out that identity. From Cheryl's earliest years, her father has patiently taught her a number of age-appropriate tasks, from tying her shoes to operating a computer and the power tools in the garage. Don conveyed great confidence in his daughter. "I know you can do it, sweetheart. Let Daddy show you again, then you can try it." He did not pressure her to perform or spotlight her failures. When Cheryl graduated from Bible school, the verse she selected to accompany her picture in the yearbook was Philippians 4:13: "I can do everything through him who gives me strength." Having learned from Don to be capable and competent in many areas, she had no trouble seeing herself as a competent child of God. As a result, Cheryl became involved in a tough inner-city ministry where her determination and confidence are paying dividends for the kingdom of God.

Did You See the Light in Those Who Parented You?

Scripture presents three vital ingredients of the parenting process: modeling, teaching, and relating. If these biblical ingredients were evident in the lives of those who parented you, your childhood home was likely bathed in God's light, allowing you to see your true identity. To the extent that these ingredients were weak or missing, your view of your identity was distorted.

1. *Modeling.* Whether or not they are aware of it, parents serve as models for their children. The only question is whether they are good or bad models. Jesus said, "In the same way, let your good deeds shine out for all to see, so that everyone will praise your heavenly Father" (Matt. 5:16, NLT). Children observe and imitate their parents' words, behaviors, and attitudes. They learn to think as their parents think, feel as their parents feel, choose what their parents choose, and act as their parents act.

What did your parental figures model for you? Was it primarily positive or negative?

2. *Teaching.* God instructed his people, "Impress [these commandments] on your children. Talk about them when you sit at home and when you walk along the road, when you lie down and when you get up" (Deut. 6:7). Parents are charged by God to teach their children the biblical principles and procedures for living. Education in the home must go beyond teaching kids how to tie shoes and complete household chores. It must include teaching them about important things such as God, faith, salvation, and obedience. Biblical teaching includes not only verbal instruction but also appropriate and timely discipline.

What did you learn from your parents about God, Christian faith, and a relationship with Jesus Christ? What did they teach you about living out the instructions of Scripture?

3. *Relating.* Parents are to love their children and relate to them as persons in a tender, caring way. Christ's command, "As I have loved you, so you must love one another" (John 13:34), must be applied in the home first. Children are people who need to be loved and cared for like people. The psalmist noted, "Children are a gift from the Lord" (Ps. 127:3, NLT). How do you handle a gift? You cherish it. Without a warm, loving, intimate relationship be-

tween parent and child, the ingredients of modeling and teaching will be ineffective in a child's life.

How did your parents relate to you as a child? Did they treat you like a responsibility, a burden, or a distraction in their lives? Did they interact with you lovingly as someone they cherished and appreciated?

SEEING THE LIGHT THROUGH YOUR PARENTS

Children who are bathed in God's light through their parents' godly example and care have a much greater opportunity to grow up seeing themselves as God sees them. Here is what the light might look like coming through loving Christian parents.

1. *Parents help their children understand they are loved and valued by God when they display an intimate relationship with Jesus Christ.* This is the ingredient of modeling at work. Parents reflect the light of Christ when they talk respectfully and reverently about him in everyday conversation, when they relate to Christ as a person instead of the head of their religion, when their behavior is patterned after what Jesus taught and how he lived.

How did the people who raised you regard Jesus Christ? Was his name uttered with reverence in your home, or was it a swear word? Was the unconditional love of Christ evident in your parents' behavior, or were their words and actions the antithesis of selflessness and caring? Were you read or told stories about Jesus in your home? Did your parents speak of their daily fellowship with Christ? Did you overhear your father or mother conversing with God in prayer as if he were there in the room? Did you hear your parents say things such as, "Isn't it wonderful that Jesus loves us and forgives us?" or "I thank God for a child like you" or "Jesus really protected us when that car ran a red light in front of us"?

2. *Parents help their children see that they are loved and valued by God when the Bible is at the center of family life.* This is the teaching

ingredient of parenting in action. The Bible is God's written Word stating who we are in him. When the Bible is a part of family life, children absorb a clearer picture of their true identity.

Parents who merely sit their children down every day, open the Bible, and preach at them are not effective teachers. Rather, the Bible becomes the basis for effective teaching when it is referred to, talked about, read, and quoted in the context of daily activities. There is some value to structured Bible activity such as a scheduled time of family devotions or planned occasions for Bible memorization projects. But formal study is effective only if the Bible is also talked about and referred to informally at other times of the week.

Parents teach volumes about the importance of Scripture by how they relate to Scripture personally. Tom and Jackie have two sons. As the boys were growing up, Tom's habit was to rise early every morning and to read a chapter from the Bible at the dining room table. He was usually done before the rest of the family awoke. But occasionally one of the boys would wander into the dining room and find Tom hunched over the Bible at the table. Tom never made a big deal about what he was doing; he did not "stage" his devotions so the boys would find him there.

When Kip, their older son, entered high school, he had to get up early to practice for swim team. One morning Tom came to the dining room to read, and there was Kip, sitting in Tom's chair and reading the Bible. Tom did not mind at all having to find a new place for his time of devotions while Kip was on the swim team.

Both sons are married today. They remember very little from family devotions in their parents' home. But they did witness what the Bible meant to their father, and they are men of the Word as a result.

How much light came into your life through the Scriptures when you were growing up? If there was a Bible in your home, was it more than just a family heirloom or a decoration on the coffee table? Did you witness one or both of your parents reading the Bible? Did they read the Bible or Bible storybooks to you? Did you sense that your parents regarded the Bible as truth, that they lived their lives by its principles? Do you remember times when Bible verses or topics were discussed informally in the context of family activities?

3. *Parents help their children discover that they are loved and valued by God when Christian fellowship is a central part of their lives.* This is a further expression of the relating ingredient of parenting. As children are introduced to an environment in which a group of believers care for and encourage one another, the love and care they receive from their parents is multiplied. As children see their parents caring for others and being cared for by others, they learn that God loves and values others as well as themselves. Furthermore, as children interact with Sunday school teachers, youth leaders, and other adult believers in a biblical fellowship, the message of their parents' lives is expanded and amplified.

How much light came into your life as a child through church involvement? Were your parents active in a Bible-believing, Christ-centered church? Were church activities a significant part of family life? Did your parents encourage you to become involved in Sunday school, vacation Bible school, youth group, or other activities in which you could relate to people your age?

HOPE FOR THE IMPERFECT HOME

Before I was married, I used to spend a lot of time at Paula's house. She had the most wonderful Christian parents. She never heard her parents argue or even raise their voices to one another. I used to think, *God, why couldn't I have had parents like Paula's, people who love each other?* My home was not a Christian home. The Bible and church were not a part of my upbringing. Furthermore, I do not remember my father hugging me, and I never saw him hug my mother. Although our family had some good times, our life was overshadowed by a steady stream of trials, tribulations, and heartaches. Many of the conflicts in our home were the result of my father's alcoholism. As a result, I grew up with a very poor perception of how much God loved and valued me.

I used to spend so much time at Paula's because I envied her. Then I realized that God had chosen my parents for me just as he had chosen Paula's parents for her. I began to see that he used even the undesirable characteristics in my parents to shape my life.

If you feel disadvantaged because of a background devoid of much light, don't be discouraged. God uses all the circumstances in our lives, good and bad, to prepare us for what he will do in us and through us. Everything that happens to us is an occasion for God to exercise his comfort and to prepare us to comfort others (see 2 Cor. 1:3-4). God used Romans 8:28 to help me get a better picture of my background: "We know that in all things God works for the good of those who love him, who have been called according to his purpose." Today I am truly thankful for my alcoholic father because God faithfully used those circumstances to shape me and to equip me to help others.

Perhaps you are coming to understand some of your parents' failures more clearly. If you are, you must first come to the point of saying, "Thank you, God, for my parents. I don't understand your reasons for allowing me to experience what I did as I grew up. But I believe you will cause all of it to work together for good."

GETTING A CLEARER PICTURE OF YOUR IDENTITY

Part of understanding who you are involves understanding who God is and experiencing his heart toward you. Reflect on the following truths about God. Take time to write your responses to the questions in a notebook or journal.

1. *God is understanding.* We read in 1 Chronicles 28:9: "Worship and serve him with your whole heart and with

a willing mind. For the Lord sees every heart and understands and knows every plan and thought" (NLT).
- What does it mean to you that God is understanding?
- What does it mean to you that God understands everything about you?

2. *God is unchanging.* We read in Malachi 3:6: "I am the Lord, and I do not change" (NLT).
   - What does it mean to you that God doesn't change?
   - What does it mean to you that God is steady, dependable, not fickle?

A second part of understanding who you are involves hearing what God says about who *you* are. Listen to God's voice speaking to you:

1. *God says, "You are complete."* We read in Colossians 2:10: "You are complete through your union with Christ" (NLT).
   - Take this verse and personalize it: "Because of Jesus Christ, I am a complete person. I am not a defect or a reject. I am complete."
   - What does it mean to you that God through his Son has made you complete—not just good enough, but complete?
   - Do you sense God's heart toward you in giving you this sense of wholeness?

2. *God says, "You are my heir."* We read in Romans 8:17: "Since we are his children, we will share his treasures—for everything God gives to his Son, Christ, is ours, too" (NLT).
   - Take this verse and personalize it: "I am God's child, and every treasure he gave to his dearly loved Son, Jesus Christ, he will also share with me."

- What does it mean to you that God shares all of his treasures with you?
- Do you sense God's heart toward you in making you his heir, his child on whom he showers blessings?

Take time to thank God for what he has revealed about himself to you. Listen to him as he speaks these words to your heart throughout the coming days and weeks. Let these truths from Scripture work their way deep into your heart and your identity.

CHAPTER 6

The Primary Artist
of Your Self-Portrait

The people who have been the primary artists of your self-portrait are your parents. And in most cases, the dominant parent has the greater influence on how you view yourself. For me, that was my father, even though I had little or no relationship with him. That may be the case for you, too. It certainly was for my friend O'Neill.

O'Neill was raised in a small town, the eldest of three children. His parents loved their children in the best way they knew how: by providing for them materially. O'Neill's father substituted hard work for fatherly affection. He never put his arm around his son, never told O'Neill he loved him or was proud of him. O'Neill's mother, who also suffered for lack of intimacy, was overly protective.

As a boy, O'Neill worked hard to earn his parents' acceptance, affection, and approval by trying to be what they wanted him to be. He was an obedient, successful son who was paraded before his younger brother and sister as a good example. He was not allowed to fight with other kids. Whenever a conflict arose, O'Neill's mother always intervened. By the time he reached junior high school, O'Neill's peers called him Lacy because they thought he was a sissy who probably wore lacy underwear.

To make matters worse, O'Neill was a chronic bed wetter until he was fifteen. His father could not understand the bed-wetting

71

and reacted with anger, accusing O'Neill of doing it purposely to spite him. Unable to go on sleepovers with other boys, O'Neill experienced increasing loneliness and feelings of inferiority. He tried the Boy Scouts, but the teasing followed him there. Lacking closeness with his father and acceptance among his friends, O'Neill was filled with rage but had no way to express it.

Then he discovered football. Good-sized, strong, and gifted, O'Neill found satisfaction in venting his anger on the field. During high school his bed-wetting problem subsided, and he made the first team in football. O'Neill finally began to receive some respect from his classmates. Largely due to O'Neill's contributions, his team went to the state play-offs. But because the person who controlled athletic awards in the region did not like O'Neill's father, my friend was overlooked when state honors were announced. The snub drove another wedge between O'Neill and his father.

At about the same time, O'Neill got involved in a church youth group where he was the big fish in a little pond. Though a Christian in name only, he became leader of the high school group, gaining acclaim from the adult sponsors. One summer at church camp he committed his life to full-time Christian service because he sensed that the adult leaders expected it of him.

O'Neill's college career began with another disappointment. A promised football scholarship at a major university was rescinded at the last moment. Angered by the rebuff, O'Neill decided to prove he could play at the major college level. He enrolled and made the team as a walk-on during his freshman year. But the head coach, who didn't like this "nice Christian boy," harassed him on and off the field, made false accusations about him, and benched him for no reason. When O'Neill angrily confronted him, the coach told him he would never play another down of football at the school. The pain of rejection from another father figure was almost more than O'Neill could bear.

O'Neill's weekends at the university were times of loneliness, rage, and depression. He cruised the highway for hours every night looking for a girl to pick up or a fight to get into. He had no close friends. He was afraid to allow anyone to get close enough to see the frightened little boy inside. He was sure no one would like him because he did not like himself. All the while, he continued to prepare himself for the ministry, even though he knew there was no substance to his Christian faith.

The summer after his junior year at the university, O'Neill heard the gospel of Christ clearly for the first time. He received Christ and expected that his life would be completely transformed. Yet nothing seemed to change. His loneliness, sense of inferiority, and rage did not go away. He was more miserable than ever. O'Neill knew that Christ was in his life, but he was discouraged that his problems had not disappeared as he had hoped they would.

During his senior year, O'Neill met and married a wonderful girl. But marriage seemed to stir up greater feelings of inferiority. He was not able to communicate with his wife at a personal level because he was afraid to let her know him. So for the first several months their marriage simply drifted along.

After college, O'Neill and his wife were hired to work at a Christian camp. It was a turning point in O'Neill's life. At the camp he met a Christian counselor who helped him understand how his distant and seemingly uncaring father had left him with a sense of mistaken identity. The deep shadows over his life from the past had kept him from enjoying a productive life as God's loved and valued child. The counselor introduced O'Neill to biblical truths that shed light on his true identity in Christ. Through the counselor's acceptance, affection, and approval of him, O'Neill began to believe that God could actually love him, value him, and find him competent.

That summer O'Neill began to see himself as God sees him. By pursuing deeper intimacy with Christ, studying the Scriptures, and seeking fellowship with loving believers, he realized that the inner portrait he had inherited from his father and others was inaccurate. O'Neill and his wife spent many hours together in Christian counseling, uncovering the wonders of their identity in Christ. The transformation was not easy, but O'Neill is finally enjoying the person God created him to be.

Today he carries no bitterness toward his father, even though the memories of his difficult childhood still move him emotionally. He has grown through his pain and has ministered to hundreds of other hurting people over the years. His gratitude is summarized in the words of Paul: "Praise be to the God and Father of our Lord Jesus Christ, the Father of compassion and the God of all comfort, who comforts us in all our troubles, so that we can comfort those in any trouble with the comfort we ourselves have received from God" (2 Cor. 1:3-4).

GROWING UP WITH AN ALCOHOLIC FATHER

O'Neill's experience parallels my own in many ways. My early relationship with my father seriously hindered the development of my sense of identity as a loved, valued, and competent child of God. Dad was an alcoholic. My school friends would joke about my dad being the town drunk. They never knew how much their jokes bothered me. Outwardly I laughed, but inside I cried.

Sometimes I would go out to the barn and find my mother lying in the manure behind the cows, knocked down so hard by my dad that she could not get up. Twice she left home because of his abuse.

When my siblings and I had friends coming over to the house, I made sure Dad could not embarrass us with his drunkenness. I would take him into the barn and literally tie him up. Then I parked the car on the far side of the silo. We would tell our friends that Dad had to go somewhere. I don't think anyone has hated someone more than I hated my father. Several times, exploding in rage, I beat him up and almost killed him.

Talk about an identity crisis—I was clueless! Because of my father's lack of respect for my mother and me, I was completely unaware that God or anyone else could see me as lovable, valuable, and competent. To compensate for the ugly inner portrait my father passed on to me, I became a pleaser. I worked harder than everyone else at chores, studies, and athletics. As a result, I excelled in studies and at sports, all the while expecting to fail in both areas.

When I entered college, a professor told me I had two things going for me: the ability to put arguments and facts together to prove a point, and tremendous determination and drive. He suggested I consider going into law. I finally saw a ray of hope for gaining the respect I had missed as a child, and my mind raced far beyond a law career. I would show my father and everyone else that I was a force to be reckoned with. I mapped out a strategy that would carry me all the way to becoming governor of Michigan in twenty-five years. Step number one was to get elected president of my college freshman class, which I soon checked off my list as accomplished.

Cocky over my newly discovered powers of logic, I decided to refute Christianity for a term project. It was my response to a run-in with an evangelistic group. Soon after starting the project, I met a group of Christian students. For more than a year I argued with them over the truth of Christianity. After looking into the evidence thoroughly, however, I realized that I could not disprove it.

But I still held out. Even if Jesus did perform miracles and had been raised from the dead, he seemed like a killjoy to me. I didn't want anyone ruining my good times. More than a year later, after tossing and turning all one night thinking about it, I gave in. I told God, "In spite of myself, I guess I believe you are real." I admitted to him that I had been wrong—sinful—and asked him to forgive me. I told him to take my life and make me more like my Christian friends.

At first I felt no better. In fact, I felt worse, wondering what I had gotten myself into. I still hated my father and struggled with the sense of inferiority and defensiveness I had grown up with. But in a matter of months I found that my life was changing. A measure of peace began to replace my constant restlessness. My explosive temper disappeared. And eventually God transformed the hatred for my father into compassion, and he used me to lead my dad to Christ before he died.

My early sense of identity was distorted in large part due to a troubled relationship with my alcoholic father. This dark portrait was a great obstacle in my life until I trusted Christ and he began to transform my perception of who I am.

A PARENT'S IMPACT

My father's inability to love me and care for me significantly hindered my capacity to develop a healthy self-portrait. That experience has led me to believe that no one is more intimately involved in the creation of your earliest inner portrait than your more dominant parent; in my case, that was my father.

When any parent fails to meet his or her children's needs for attention, acceptance, appreciation, support, encouragement, affection, respect, security, comfort, and approval—those children are hindered in seeing themselves as a loving God sees them. It is unrealistic to think that children of either sex can gain an accurate first view of who God created them to be when the parent does not fulfill his or her God-ordained role.

You do not need to be reminded of the breakdown of the American family and the disappearance of loving and supportive parents—especially fathers—in our culture. A dwindling number of children grow up in homes where the father is present and active in the nurture of the children. And when the father abdicates his role, either by leaving physically through divorce or separation or emotionally by elevating his career or hobbies above his family, the children are often robbed of a sense of who they are.

The problem seems to have begun with the Industrial Revolution and the urbanization of society. When ours was an agrarian, rural culture, the father figure was central and dynamic in the American home and in child development. Since his "career" was the family farm, the father had greater contact with the children, particularly since the children often worked alongside him as soon as they were able. Furthermore, the lack of outside distractions like television, home video games, and the Internet allowed for family-centered entertainment in the evenings. Dad, Mom, and the kids worked together and played together.

My father's inability to love me and care for me significantly hindered my capacity to develop a healthy self-portrait.

Since previous generations were more deeply committed to biblical values, the rural family often prayed together, read the Bible together, and attended church together. Thanks to this close working, playing, and worshiping relationship with both father and mother, children received a much clearer view of their true identity under God.

Today most fathers and many mothers work outside the home, and children rarely get to see their parents' workplaces. Some children don't even know what their fathers do at work, let alone have the opportunity to work with him. Dad may see his kids at breakfast or dinner, but in many homes he leaves before they get up and does not return until late evening. Some fathers travel all week and want to be left alone all weekend. Their careers and hobbies, instead of bringing them closer to their children, as was the case in the agrarian culture, serve only to push their children away.

A large majority of Americans today have been touched by the problem of an ineffective father relationship. It is an epidemic with many causes and far-reaching consequences. If I had the power to change one cultural phenomenon, it would be to correct the problem of the absentee, passive, or uninvolved parents in the American home—especially the father.

Traditionally, girls have a closer nurturing relationship with their mothers than boys have with either their fathers or mothers. Although boys and girls need positive input from both parents, it seems that boys suffer greater loss when a father is missing or uninvolved. As a result, girls tend to have a better sense of identity than boys do.

A friend of mine became aware of this discrepancy when he was personnel director for Campus Crusade for Christ. In his role he interviewed college graduates for Crusade staff positions. He observed that female applicants consistently manifested a healthier, more confident sense of identity than did male applicants. As a group, the males were less sure of who they were. All of the applicants were considered the cream of the crop: student body officers, top athletes, outstanding scholars. Yet my friend found the males to be consistently less confident than the females.

MEN DEPRIVED OF A FATHER'S NURTURE

If you are a man, your perception of your identity has probably been significantly influenced by your relationship with your father, especially your relationship when you were a child. Did you grow up with a dad in your home? If so, was your father actively involved in your life as a nurturer, disciplinarian, instructor, and friend? Or were you, like O'Neill and me, the victim of an unaffectionate, abusive, or alcoholic father who led you to feel unloved, devalued, and incompetent as a person? Whether you were deprived of your father because he was physically absent or just emotionally absent, your identity has most likely been shaped by the lack of his involvement in your life.

1. *Father-deprived men grow up with a weak sense of masculinity.* Lacking a nurturing relationship with their dads, they are left to themselves to discover what it means to be a man. Most men try to compensate for this inadequacy. They do so in a variety of ways.

Some men try to prove their masculinity through achievement. If a man can make more money or climb the corporate ladder faster than the next guy, he thinks he has displayed his masculinity.

Other men try to prove their masculinity through competition. The guy who wins, whether in checkers or golf or softball, is clearly "the best man." This was a big issue for me growing up. I was a fierce competitor, and I hated to lose. It was my way of showing I was a man.

Men who desperately need to win often pass on their warped sense of masculinity to their children. When nine-year-old Joel plays video games with his father, the activity always ends with Joel running to his room in tears. Joel's daddy cannot play for fun, allowing his young son an advantage. He has to win, and Joel will grow up with the same compulsion as a result.

There is much more to your identity as a child of God than being "a man." If you find yourself continually striving to prove yourself, you may be suffering from a lack of nurturing from your father. The chapters ahead will help you experience the transformation of seeing yourself as God sees you.

2. *Father-deprived men often grow up with hostility toward women.* This may arise because a boy's mother or mother figure tries to compensate for the absence or passivity of the father. As a boy nears the age of ten or eleven, however, he begins to resist a domi-

nant, smothering mother. He may love his mother, but her dominance may cause him to withdraw from her physically and emotionally to escape her suffocating attention. In adulthood the man's anger toward his mother may transfer to other women.

A corollary to hostility toward the mother is the fear of being dominated by any woman. As an adult, a man may vow never to allow a woman to control him. Subconsciously he may avoid emotional intimacy even while pursuing physical intimacy. As a husband, he may become compliant and silent or angry and distant. Any of the above behaviors bring serious problems to a marriage.

3. *Father-deprived men often fear deep relationships with other men.* Studies reveal that a high percentage of men today have no same-sex friends with whom they can share at an intimate level. After they discuss the weather, sports, the stock market, interest rates, and cars, many men have nothing to talk about. A healthy father-son relationship is the training ground and model for intimate male relationships in adulthood. Men who did not experience an intimate relationship with their fathers are ill-equipped to develop the same with other men. They may also fear that close friendship with another man borders on homosexuality. On the other hand, the absence of a nurturing father figure turns some men toward homosexuality. It seems that the need for a relationship with a substitute father, along with either fear of or hostility toward women, leaves some men vulnerable to a homosexual relationship.

If you are a man and if some of the problems presented here have plagued you, it may indicate that your inner portrait still suffers from the lack of a close relationship with your father. If you are a woman, perhaps you recognize some of these problems in your husband or fiancé. In either case, I encourage you to keep reading to gain insight on how to transform that faulty picture into a true representation of who you are.

WOMEN DEPRIVED OF A FATHER'S NURTURE

Women who grew up in homes where the father was absent physically or emotionally are often susceptible to a similar set of problems.

1. Father-deprived women may distrust men. When a female does not enjoy a warm, loving, affectionate relationship with her father, she may enter adulthood somewhat distrustful of men in general. Since her father failed to meet her deep emotional and relational needs, she may subconsciously expect other men to fail her, so she keeps a safe distance.

Claudia is a thirty-one-year-old insurance agent with everything going her way. In addition to having a striking appearance, she is successful in business and has her own home, a nice car, and many friends. Claudia is active in her church and shares her faith through her example and spoken testimony. Everyone says about Claudia, "She is a wonderful woman. The only thing she needs is a husband."

Claudia says she would like to be married and have children. She attracts many eligible bachelors her age through work and church. She dates frequently, and most of the men she goes out with call again. But after two or three dates with the same guy, just about the time he is thinking the relationship could get serious, Claudia begins to pull away. Even if she likes the man, she finds herself doing things that will discourage his advances. She purposely avoids returning his phone calls. She is intentionally late for a date or stands him up. She gets moody or critical when around him. Before long, the man gets discouraged and stops calling. Claudia is secretly relieved. She tells her friends, "We just didn't hit it off." Soon the cycle begins again with another eager suitor, and it always ends the same way.

Evelyn, the pastor's wife, watched Claudia go through the cycle several times. She invited Claudia to lunch one day and began asking about her family, particularly her father. Claudia revealed

81

that she never had a close relationship with her father, who openly preferred her two older brothers to her. Over a period of months, Evelyn's wise and loving counsel helped Claudia see that her experience at home was being lived out in each of her dating relationships. Claudia kept her father at a distance to avoid the pain of his rejection. She was doing the same with the men who came into her life, even though she yearned for the security of a marriage relationship.

Women like Claudia bring their distrust into the marriage relationship. While going through the motions of intimacy, they may be unable to trust their husbands to meet their deepest needs. As they become more aloof and distrustful, the strain on the marriage may lead to separation or divorce.

Sometimes the general distrust of men leads to an all-out hostility toward men. The problem is usually rooted in long-standing bitterness toward a distant father, a bitterness that is displaced to other men in her life.

2. Father-deprived women may solicit inappropriate affection and attention from other men. If a woman's need for affection and attention from her father was not met when she was a girl, she may compensate by trying to get affection and attention from other men, often in inappropriate ways. Some extremely promiscuous women have acknowledged that they were not enticed by the sexual activity in itself. Rather, they gave their bodies away in exchange for the affection they craved. Girls who have experienced positive, warm relationships with their fathers at home are usually better equipped emotionally to say no to sexual temptation.

How much light came through your father or mother to illuminate your true identity? If you are like many people, your perception of who you are is different from God's view of who you are because your father or mother did not provide a sufficient amount of light for you. I say this not to disparage your parents but to help you understand that any sense of identity you may have missed from your dad or your mom can be reclaimed. No matter how bad your home life may have been, you have the opportunity to see yourself as God sees you. And his view is the one you want.

GETTING A CLEARER PICTURE OF YOUR IDENTITY

Part of understanding who you are involves understanding who God is and experiencing his heart toward you. Reflect on the following truths about God. Take time to write your responses to the questions in a notebook or journal.

1. *God is your Father.* We read in Psalm 103:13: "The Lord is like a father to his children" (NLT).
   - What does it mean to you that God is like a father to his children?
   - What does it mean to you that God—the Father of our Lord Jesus Christ—is *your* Father?

2. *God is tender.* We read in Psalm 103:13: "The Lord is like a father to his children, tender and compassionate to those who fear him" (NLT).
   - What does it mean to you that God is tender?
   - What does it mean to you that a tender God calls you his child and welcomes you into his arms?

A second part of understanding who you are involves hearing what God says about who *you* are. Listen to God's voice speaking to you:

1. *God says, "You are valuable."* We read in Luke 12:24: "Look at the ravens. They don't need to plant or harvest or put food in barns because God feeds them. And you are far more valuable to him than any birds!" (NLT).

- Take this verse and personalize it: "God values birds enough to nurture them and take care of their needs. Since I am more valuable to God than the birds, I can trust him to take care of my needs too."
- What does it mean to you that God values you?
- Do you sense God's heart toward you as he assures you of his willingness to nurture you?

2. *God says, "You are my child."* We read in Galatians 4:7: "Now you are no longer a slave but God's own child" (NLT).

- Take this verse and personalize it: "I am God's child. Even if my father deserted me, I belong to God."
- What does it mean to you that God has made you his very own child?
- Do you sense God's heart toward you in embracing you into his family, in selecting you to be his child?

Take time to thank God for what he has revealed about himself to you. Listen to him as he speaks these words to your heart throughout the coming days and weeks. Let these truths from Scripture work their way deep into your heart and your identity.

CHAPTER 7

The Influence from
Outside Your Home

W e all grew up in a world that was at times apathetic and cruel toward us. God loves each of us completely and unconditionally. But people sometimes make us feel very unloved. God values us so much that he sent his Son to die for us. The words and actions of others occasionally cause us to view ourselves as worthless. And our inner portrait suffers as a result.

As I grew up, my perception of my identity was shaped not only by my father but also by several other significant influences: people at school, the culture, and religion. These three elements also affected your inner self-portrait, and in some cases, as I discovered, the influence was more negative than positive.

THE IMPACT OF PEOPLE AT SCHOOL

I was born left-handed. But when I was in the second grade, my teacher tried to make me switch to using my right hand. She would sit me down at a table spread with blocks, instructing, "Build a house out of these blocks." Then she stood over me as I began my task. If I reached out with my left hand, she smacked it with a ruler and said, "Stop and think it through. Do it with your right hand." I was terrified and confused. I was only doing what came naturally, but I was severely punished for it. Can you imagine how this colored my self-portrait? I began to think I was defective, a factory reject.

This traumatic experience caused me to develop a speech impediment. Whenever I became frightened, anxious, or tired—usually at school—I stuttered. My stuttering was a great embarrassment to me. In the fifth grade I was told to memorize and recite the Gettysburg Address. I was so nervous when I stood up that I began to stutter. In front of the entire class, my teacher demanded, "Say it! Say it! Stop stuttering, and say it!" Mortified in front of my friends, I ran out of the classroom crying.

Because my parents' education stopped at the second grade, they had never learned grammar. As a result, I did not pick up very good grammar at home. If my English teachers emphasized correct grammar, it never got through to me. Somehow I got by. But when I entered college, my down-home grammar caught up with me, and I again became the object of my instructors' ridicule. I was embarrassed to speak up in class. One day in freshman English, the professor asked me, "Where's Bob?" I said, "He doesn't feel good." In front of everyone, the professor corrected me: "Mr. McDowell, you mean 'Bob doesn't feel *well*.'" I looked at her perplexed, wondering what the big deal was. To me it seemed just as well to say good! Experiences like these further solidified my perception that I was an inferior human being.

Bryan had a similar experience at school, but one of his teachers helped to reverse this process in his life. Bryan grew up in an unhappy home. His mother deserted the family when he was quite young. His father was away from home in the military, so Bryan spent most of his young life with his grandparents. Having been deserted by his parents, he felt unloved and unwanted.

Bryan's first few years of school were miserable. Misbehaving just to gain attention, he was branded a problem kid, and he lived up to that label. One year when he moved up to the next grade, he was greeted at the classroom door by a very wise teacher. She looked him straight in the eye and said, "Bryan, I've heard all about you, but I don't believe a word of it!" That day was a turning point in his young life, Bryan recalls. Someone saw something of value and promise in him. Someone believed in him. If you had teachers, coaches, grandparents, or other significant adults like Bryan's teacher in your life, you were blessed and your sense of identity benefited.

The negative influence of teachers and classmates often works against the positive influence a child may receive at home. Consider the red-haired girl who was told at home how cute she was. The day she started school a classmate taunted her as Carrot Top. Another one nicknamed her Freckle Face. She was crushed at the way her new friends turned what she thought were beautiful characteristics into the butt of ridicule. Or consider the boy who had been affirmed as competent by loving parents, only to be ridiculed at school as clumsy and slow because his coordination was not as developed as that of his peers.

Children can be cruel to each other. They have a way of magnifying a tiny fault or blemish into a major issue. Their name-calling and taunts can mar an inner portrait parents have carefully guarded. No doubt as a child you were the butt of the jokes and barbs of some of your so-called friends. Every snub, every unkind remark added another unsightly scratch to your inner portrait, causing you to doubt your intrinsic value. Your perception needs to be transformed to how God sees you.

I am living proof that God can transform an inner portrait marred by the abuse and neglect of teachers and peers. After I became a Christian, I transferred to Wheaton College, a Christian school. The more I grew in my faith, the more I struggled over the challenge to give myself entirely to the Lord. I resisted the challenge because I thought he might want me to go into Christian ministry, which meant only one thing to me: public speaking. At that time my poor grammar and stuttering problem were still very evident. As a result, it seemed to me that giving "everything" to God was giving very little he could use.

Finally I said, "God, I don't think I have any speaking talents or other gifts you can use in ministry. I stutter when I'm scared, and I speak horrible English. I have all these limitations, so you surely don't want me in ministry. But if you can take these limitations and make something out of them, I will serve you the rest of my life."

In the hands of God, who knows no limitations, my weaknesses have become strengths. I have been privileged to speak about Christ to millions of people in over half the countries of the world. When I began to see myself as God sees me instead of clinging to the portrait passed on to me by my parents, teachers, and peers, I was able to live beyond my limitations.

After all these years, I still struggle a little with proper grammar when I speak and write. Every time I address a crowd or begin work on a new book, I am aware of both my weakness and the grace of God. But I am no longer intimidated by the obstacles that loomed so large early in my Christian life. My sense of identity has been transformed. I am not a defective reject. I am not a hopeless stutterer. I am a beloved child of God, redeemed by the blood of Christ and equipped by the Spirit for his service. Today I can say with all honesty, "Thank you, God, for the parents you gave me and the childhood I experienced." Even the difficulties I faced growing up have helped shape what I am today. I can identify with Paul's encouraging words in Philippians 1:6: "He who began a good work in you will carry it on to completion until the day of Christ Jesus."

THE IMPACT OF AN IMPERSONAL CULTURE

Picture the scene. Darlene arrives home from work at 5:45. She walks through the house and calls out, "Hi, kids, I'm home." A mumbled reply drifts out of fourteen-year-old Casey's room, where he is engrossed in a game on his computer. Darlene knows Edie is home because she can hear her daughter's favorite video blaring from the eleven-year-old's room. Darlene quickly changes out of her suit into jeans and a shirt, then opens up her laptop computer to finish off a few items of business in the family room while listening to music from the entertainment center.

My sense of identity has been transformed. I am not a defective reject. I am not a hopeless stutterer. I am a beloved child of God, redeemed by the blood of Christ and equipped by the Spirit for his service.

Joel, Darlene's husband, arrives home from work about thirty minutes later. It was his turn to pick up dinner, and he opted for take-out Chinese food. He places the steaming boxes on the kitchen counter and pulls out four plates and forks. When he returns from changing his clothes, three plates are gone and the boxes are half empty. Joel fills a plate and joins Darlene in the family room. He turns off the music and flips on the television to a news station, easing up the volume to drown out the noise of the computer game and video from the kids' rooms, where they have retreated with heaping plates of kung pao chicken and shrimp lo mein. Darlene pecks away at the computer in between bites of food, glances at the news, and snatches of conversation with Joel.

Casey emerges from his room long enough to load the dishwasher and put away the leftovers—his job for the week. Then he is back in his room to grind out some homework before returning to computer games. Edie snaps on her computer to dig up some information on Betsy Ross from the Internet. But she is quickly distracted into a chat room where her friends, whom she has never met in person, talk every night.

As soon as Darlene is done on the laptop computer, Joel goes on-line to check his E-mail and stock portfolio. Darlene slips in and out of the kids' rooms for a brief visit, then settles down to watch her favorite television shows. Joel entertains himself with thirty-six holes of computer golf. Sometime between 10:00 and 11:30 P.M., all the computers, TVs, VCRs, and stereos in the house are shut down as the family readies for bed. Tomorrow night will look about the same as tonight—only it will be Darlene's turn to stop on the way home from work to pick up the family dinner.

This scenario may not look much like the home you grew up in, but it resembles a large number of homes in our country today. A generation or two ago, culture was a ring of influence largely kept outside the family and perhaps the church. Many children grew up somewhat sheltered from immorality, pornography, violence, and secularism because they usually had to go somewhere outside the home to encounter it. Today the world has moved into our living rooms, family rooms, and bedrooms in the form of cable and satellite television and the Internet. Everything you and your children could possibly see and hear in our culture—including the dark realms of pornography and the occult—is available at the flip of a switch or a few clicks on the mouse.

Even in Christian homes where television and Internet access are monitored by parents, kids are strongly influenced by the culture. Even G- and PG-rated sitcoms, dramas, movies, educational programs, and Web sites bring a secular worldview into our homes. Chat rooms and E-mail link us and our kids with people whose values may be contrary to ours. The culture that at one time could be kept at a distance now cohabits with the average American family. You likely grew up during this subtle and insidious transition.

To whatever extent you were exposed to it while growing up, the non-Christian culture influenced your perception of your identity. Along with your parents and other significant adults in your life, culture communicated to you who you are. But the way culture sees you and the way God sees you are as different as night and day. Non-Christian culture cannot help but communicate non-Christian values. In our culture, people are often loved and valued conditionally instead of unconditionally. The world cottons to beautiful, well-educated, physically fit, successful, and affluent persons while minimizing or ignoring those without a health-club body, white-collar occupation, or swelling bank account.

For example, let's say that Celeste, a twenty-eight-year-old professional accountant, grew up with few restrictions on her television viewing. She watched cartoons by the hour as a child, sitcoms and dramas as a teen, and soap operas and "mature" videos as a young adult. Along with the programs she watched, Celeste also absorbed literally hours and hours of commercial messages every year. She attended church and professed a Christian faith, but she had no time to cultivate a devotional life due to her obsession with television.

What did the media communicate to Celeste about her identity? By her early teen years, Celeste had quietly realized that she would likely never have a serious boyfriend, let alone a loving, devoted husband. Large-boned and perpetually overweight, she knew she could not compete with the supermodel types who always got the big hunks in the movies, television, and commercials. "Big girls" are around for laughs, not for romance. It is not surprising that Celeste saw herself as the media saw her: unattractive and unlovable. For that reason, she struggled to believe that God could love her, effectively neutralizing her Christian growth and witness. Celeste's desperation for affection led her into sexual promiscuity with another "misfit," a man she would never consider marrying.

Like the sun's ultraviolet rays that affect exposed skin, culture made some kind of an impression on how you perceive yourself. You may have been "burned" from excessive exposure, as Celeste was. Perhaps yours was a non-Christian home where secular values and ungodly practices were not censored, leaving you with a twisted sense of your value to God. Or perhaps a milder case of exposure to the culture in a Christian environment has discolored your inner portrait only slightly. If your self-perception reflects how the world sees you, you are a candidate for transformation.

THE IMPACT OF RELIGIOUS EXPERIENCE

It may seem contradictory to say that your past Christian religious experience may have contributed to an inaccurate perception of your identity. After all, what better place to discover how God sees us than in a place where his Word is taught and where his people fellowship? But unfortunately not all spiritual leaders and teachers correctly represent God's view of our value to him.

Tom began attending church youth group activities with his friends when he was in junior high school. This particular church took a liberal view of Scripture and the deity of Christ, so Tom's first impression of Christianity was colored by this view. Tom learned that he was a product of the evolutionary process, that "God" was more a force than a person, and that God loved and valued him only as much as he loved and valued himself. For all Tom knew, this was the gospel. Only after he encountered a vibrant group of evangelical Christians as an adult did Tom realize that his early religious experience was not Christian at all. He had never clearly perceived how God saw him. Tom's assessment of his identity needed a radical transformation.

Janet was educated in a Christian school that was Bible-centered and very proud of it. She learned the Ten Commandments word-for-word as a first grader. The teacher drummed into the children that they must obey God's commands or he would punish them. The theme of legalism and performance-based righteousness pervaded the Bible curriculum of the school. Janet grew into adulthood with a warped view of God and herself. As long as she toed the line and performed her Christian duties, God loved her and cared for her. But if her performance lagged, God would be after her with a heavenly switch. God loved her when she obeyed. God valued her when she performed. She was told that the message was straight from the Bible, so who could doubt its validity? The pressure to conform eventually got to Janet. When she was a teenager, she rebelled against her church, her Christian family, and the God who she assumed had little use for an imperfect servant like her.

The Bible clearly reveals how God sees us. He loves us as persons created in his image. He values us to the point that he sacrificed his Son to redeem us. Sadly, however, some churches and Christian leaders misrepresent God's view by overemphasizing and/or underemphasizing facets of his character. In Janet's case, the relentless focus on Christian obedience and righteousness obliterated God's compassion, forgiveness, and unconditional love. She saw herself as a sinner in the hands of an angry God, desperately trying but continually failing to measure up to his standard.

My intention here is not to make you suspicious of your church, your pastor, or your Bible study leader. Most evangelical churches and leaders prayerfully seek to "proclaim . . . the whole will of God" (Acts 20:27). But no church or leader is perfect. Your perception of true identity may be somewhat clouded as a result of some oversights in teaching and doctrine among those who served as your spiritual mentors. You may have inherited from your religious experience a portrait that needs to be transformed.

Throughout your personal history, people and circumstances have been telling you who you are. Your sense of true identity may be many miles or only a few feet from how God sees you, depending on the source and biblical validity of those messages. In order to transform your inner portrait to the one God holds, you must begin to look through his eyes.

GETTING A CLEARER PICTURE OF YOUR IDENTITY

Part of understanding who you are involves understanding who God is and experiencing his heart toward you. Reflect on the following truths about God. Take time to write your responses to the questions in a notebook or journal.

> 1. *God is truth.* We read in Psalm 31:5: "Redeem me, O Lord, the God of truth."
> - What does it mean to you that God is truth?
> - What does it mean to you that the God who is truth—the God who cannot lie to you—says you are lovable, valuable, and competent?

> 2. *God is wise.* We read in Romans 16:27: "To God, who alone is wise, be the glory forever through Jesus Christ" (NLT).
> - What does it mean to you that God is wise?
> - What does it mean to you that God—who alone is wise—loves you just the way you are, finds you valuable just because you are, and makes you competent just because you are his child?

A second part of understanding who you are involves hearing what God says about who *you* are. Listen to God's voice speaking to you:

1. *God says, "I do not condemn you."* We read in Romans
   8:1: "So now there is no condemnation for those who
   belong to Christ Jesus" (NLT).
   - Take this verse and personalize it: "I belong to Christ
     Jesus, and as a result, I am not condemned."
   - What does it mean to you that God has made you his
     own and that because you belong to him, you are to-
     tally free from condemnation?
   - Do you sense God's heart toward you in promising
     not to condemn you?

2. *God says, "You are my friend."* We read in John 15:15: "I
   no longer call you servants, because a master doesn't
   confide in his servants. Now you are my friends, since I
   have told you everything the Father told me" (NLT).
   - Take this verse and personalize it: "I am God's friend.
     He tells me everything that his Father tells him."
   - What does it mean to you that you are God's
     friend—not just his creation, but his friend?
   - Do you sense God's heart toward you as he draws you
     toward himself in friendship?

Take time to thank God for what he has revealed about himself to
you. Listen to him as he speaks these words to your heart throughout the coming days and weeks. Let these truths from Scripture
work their way deep into your heart and your identity.

The Basis of Your
True Identity

CHAPTER 8

Foundation of True Identity

Susan, who was involved in full-time Christian ministry, found it nearly impossible to carry on her work. She was paralyzed by a deep sense of unworthiness at the thought of assuming the leadership roles that were demanded of her position. She felt so out of place in a Christian organization, as if she did not fit in among co-workers with such high moral standards. She was convinced that she would be demoted or fired if anyone found out about her past.

After several sessions with a Christian counselor, Susan was finally able to talk about the repulsive activities in which she had been involved before becoming a Christian. Then it all spilled out—the deep hurt, fear, and anguish she had buried after numerous illicit affairs, an abortion, and a homosexual relationship. Susan's behavior had changed dramatically since she became a Christian. But her inner portrait had not changed. God had redeemed her and forgiven her, but she still saw herself as morally bankrupt, and her poor sense of identity seriously hindered her growth and ministry.

Susan is representative of so many of the people I meet. They have committed their lives to Christ, but they cannot seem to make any headway in the Christian life. Defeated and discouraged, they have tried seemingly everything. They pray harder and longer. They get involved in more Christian activities. They make greater commitments and try to do better. Yet they continue to spin their wheels. And they don't know why.

I believe people like Susan live in frustration because they are treating their problems symptomatically instead of dealing with the root cause. It is like remodeling an old house that has a cracked and crumbling foundation. You can try to make the house livable by adding new paint and wallpaper, laying new carpet, and buying nice furniture. But the floors and ceilings will continue to sag, and the walls will eventually fall in if you fail to replace the damaged foundation.

Similarly, aggressive Bible study and prayer are necessary to Christian maturity, and involvement in Christian service and sharing your faith are important. But if you fail to see yourself as God sees you, your shaky foundation will render much of your attempts at growth ineffective. Who you are is not a result of what you do, so you cannot *do* your way to a more accurate sense of identity. What you do proceeds from who you are. If you want your activity as a disciple of Christ to be meaningful, you must gain a clearer picture of your true identity.

THREE PILLARS OF THE FOUNDATION

What makes up the foundation of your true identity? I introduced three pillars—you are lovable, valuable, and competent—in chapter 3. In the remaining chapters I want to help you lock onto these key pillars to the point that you are literally transformed by them. Only when you see yourself as God sees you will you be able to experience the fulfillment and peace he created you to enjoy.

Pillar 1: You are lovable. You may have grown up feeling ignored, unwanted, despised, or even hated. The people who conveyed that image to you were in error. God created you in his image and loves you as his own child. God makes no mistakes. If he loves you—and he does—you are eternally lovable. It is essential that you see yourself as lovable because that is how God sees you.

Pillar 2: You are valuable. Anyone who communicated to you that you are worthless or unimportant was deluded. God gave up his dear Son to reconcile you to himself. If God gave such a ransom, you are indeed infinitely valuable. It is essential that you see yourself as valuable because that is how God sees you.

Pillar 3: You are competent. Perhaps you were always the last person to complete an important task or to be chosen for a softball team. As a result, you view yourself as incompetent, unreliable, or untrustworthy. You may not be the most talented, but God has gifted you and committed to you the supreme ministry of being his light in the world. If he is ready to trust you with a task of eternal proportions, you are thoroughly competent. It is essential that you see yourself as competent because that is how God sees you.

Transforming your sense of identity is a matter of accepting and acting on what is already true.

The more clearly you see yourself as lovable, valuable, and competent, the better equipped you are to deal with life and all its complexities. This is not a matter of positive thinking. I am not suggesting that you "visualize" these three vital traits until they are true of you. You are *already* lovable, valuable, and capable. That's how God made you.

Transforming your sense of identity is a matter of accepting and acting on what is already true. As these pillars become anchored in your consciousness, you will be better prepared to withstand the trouble, trauma, and tragedy that are a part of human life.

YOU ARE LOVABLE: A SENSE OF BELONGING

Linda was abandoned at a stranger's front door as a toddler and raised by foster parents. She grew into adulthood assuming that she was not worth loving. Her birth mother had thrown her away, making Linda feel unwanted and unloved. Her sense of identity was weakened by a lack of belonging.

We all need to sense that we belong to someone. We feel that we belong when others willingly meet our needs for affection, acceptance, respect, and approval. Belonging is what we sense when we know someone loves us unconditionally just as we are. Many psychologists agree that the single most important factor for developing a healthy personality is knowing we are loved by others.

The world is full of people like Linda, people who have suffered greatly from a lack of unconditional love. But just about everyone has sensed a lack of belonging at some level. The love we received from others was imperfect because the people loving us were imperfect. At the very least, we all experienced conditional love and acceptance that communicated, "I love you because . . ." or "I will love you if. . . ." Such a message puts belonging on a performance basis. The ongoing threat is that if we do not perform to certain standards, we will not be loved. Conditional love leaves our basic hunger to belong unsatisfied.

How can our false perception of being unlovable be transformed into the picture God has of us? By reversing the process that created the false perception in the first place. For example, lacking a sense of belonging, Linda has a heightened need for affection. She needs to cultivate healthy relationships with family and friends, relationships in which she is able to give and receive affection through loving words, deeds, and touch. Similarly, she must place herself with people who accept her as she is, respect her as a person, and approve of her. Such an environment affirms the reality that has been blocked from her view: that she is lovable and deserves affection, acceptance, respect, and approval. We will talk more about transforming an unclear sense of belonging in Chapter 10, "A New Sense of Being Loved."

YOU ARE VALUABLE: A SENSE OF WORTHINESS

Jim has reached the pinnacle of success in his profession. He has written many books, and he lectures about his field of expertise around the world. Jim drives an expensive sports car, owns a large suburban home, and gives generously to his church and other charities. His peers view him as extremely successful and self-assured.

But when you get to know Jim well, you learn that he is fearful and insecure. It is this insecurity that has driven him to his positions of success. But it may also drive him to despair because his wife has threatened divorce if he does not do something about his workaholic tendencies.

Jim is suffering from a case of mistaken identity. He considers himself to be of little value apart from his business achievement. When Jim was a child, his home life was unpredictable and often painful. His alcoholic father would beat him for no apparent reason. Sometimes when Jim's mother was out of town, Dad took Jim with him to the tavern and locked him in the pickup. Dad often did not reappear until daylight. The man once sold Jim's bicycle and used the money for liquor. Jim never knew what his father would do next. As a teenager, he determined to insulate himself from such insecurity by becoming as successful and wealthy as he could.

Most children idealize their parents, lifting them to a pedestal and regarding them as perfect. So when children's need for love, security, attention, and comfort goes unmet, they take the blame personally. They reason something like this: "Mom and Dad can do no wrong, so they would love me if I was worth it. Since they don't love me, I must not be worthy of their love and care." As a result, children will often compensate for the sense of unworthiness by earning the love and attention they crave through their accomplishments outside the home, as Jim did.

People like Jim are all around us today. They see themselves as having little intrinsic value because, in effect, someone told them they were worthless human beings. This message comes through clearly when the basic needs for security, attention, and comfort go unmet. Children who grow up feeling unsafe because of a parent's abuse or neglect deduce that they are not worth caring for. Children whose parents fail to give them loving attention feel they are less than important. Children whose hurts and disappointments go uncomforted by the adults in their life sense they have little value. Like Jim, these children come into adulthood with an inner portrait that is captioned "unworthy."

In order to rebuild this pillar of the foundation, needs that went unmet during the formative years must be given attention. People like Jim need to seek out believers who will meet their needs for security, attention, and comfort in a healthy, caring way. We will explore this strategy in detail in chapter 11, "A New Sense of Worth."

YOU ARE COMPETENT: A SENSE OF CONFIDENCE

God created everyone with certain abilities and competencies. Every human being is able to say, "I am capable of making worthwhile contributions to others. I can do something." You may wonder, "But what about the quadriplegic and the victim of brain damage and the person locked in a coma? What can they do?" Those who are physically disabled can use their minds. Those who are mentally disabled may still be able to perform helpful tasks. And even the person who is physically and mentally incapacitated serves to prompt others to caring and concern, which is its own brand of capability. This pillar of true identity is optimized, of course, in the life of the believer, who is gifted by God for ministry at a spiritual level.

In an ideal environment, children grow up with a healthy sense of competence. The encouragement, support, and appreciation of loving parents sparks them to try new things and to overcome difficulties. Kids hear the story *The Little Engine That Could* and come to believe, "I think I can, I think I can." With a solid base of encouragement and support, children learn to persevere, succeeding in some areas and striving to improve in others.

Parents play an important role in developing children's sense of competence. Think about babies learning to walk. With the help of their parents, they take their first halting steps, then fall. Hearing their parents' approval and encouragement, the toddlers try again, eventually taking many successive steps before falling again. Their parents smile and applaud and say, "Good try! You can do it!" Before long the toddlers are walking everywhere.

But what would you think of a parent who discouraged a child from walking? Baby pulls himself up on unsteady legs, and Dad pushes him down again, saying something like, "You'll never learn to walk, so don't even try." Who could be so cruel as to block a child's attempt to walk? It is unthinkable. Yet many children grow up with a similar kind of negative input.

Eight-year-old Sonny was not athletically gifted, but he loved baseball. He practiced pitching hour after hour by tossing a tennis ball against the garage door. Then he tossed fly balls high into the air to develop skills in catching. When Sonny misplaced his tennis ball, he used a lemon off the backyard tree. Sonny begged his father to play catch with him, but his dad agreed only occasionally, and then somewhat reluctantly.

When Sonny turned nine, he bugged his dad until he agreed to take him to Little League tryouts at the local park. Sonny was so excited at the prospect of signing up to play that he was especially wild with his practice throws. Before the tryout session was over, his dad said, "Come on, Sonny, we're going home. You're not any good at baseball."

Sonny's frail confidence in his limited ability was shattered. It took him many years to recover a sense of competence at doing anything well. Self-doubt still plagues him as an adult.

When parents do not encourage and support the endeavors of their children, kids grow up with a diminished sense of competence. When children's efforts are not appreciated by the adults in their lives, they wonder if they did something wrong. Without positive strokes, they are not as eager to try again.

Twenty-year-old Amanda is an attractive woman who also battles self-doubt. Much of her lack of confidence originated during childhood competition with her sister Mary. Mary always did everything right, while Amanda never seemed to please her parents. The conclusion Amanda reached was that she was inept and incompetent and that her parents did not love her as much as they loved Mary. Amanda still sees herself that way as an adult. She anticipates the rejection of others when she makes a mistake, so she resists trying new things.

Sonny, Amanda, and people like them were robbed of a valid sense of their competence, and they still suffer from it today. In order to transform this pillar of their identity, they need to be in an environment where their efforts are encouraged, supported, and appreciated. We will talk more about these needs and how they can be met in Chapter 12, "A New Sense of Competence."

God created every person to be lovable, valuable, and competent. If these pillars of true identity are not affirmed during children's developmental years and if the vital needs associated with these pillars are not met by those closest to them, the children will grow up with a warped picture of their identity. In our culture, people often tend to compensate for a weak sense of belonging or worthiness by overachieving in the area of competence. They may become workaholics in a frantic attempt to earn the love and approval they missed early in their lives.

To whatever extent you were denied the clear representation of who you are, you need to be transformed. The next several chapters will help you move through this process.

GETTING A CLEARER PICTURE OF YOUR IDENTITY

Part of understanding who you are involves understanding who God is and experiencing his heart toward you. Reflect on the following truths about God. Take time to write your responses to the questions in a notebook or journal.

1. *God is good.* We read in Psalm 86:5: "O Lord, you are so good, so ready to forgive, so full of unfailing love for all who ask your aid" (NLT).
   - What does it mean to you that God is good?
   - What does it mean to you that a good God—a God who is not capable of any deceit—finds you lovable?

2. *God is fair.* We read in Psalm 119:137: "O Lord, you are righteous, and your decisions are fair" (NLT).
   - What does it mean to you that God is righteous and fair?
   - What does it mean to you that this fair God sees you as valuable and competent?

A second part of understanding who you are involves hearing what God says about who *you* are. Listen to God's voice speaking to you:

1. *God says, "You are precious."* We read in Isaiah 43:4: "You are precious to me. You are honored, and I love you" (NLT).
   - Take this verse and personalize it: "I am precious to God. He loves me and gives me honor."
   - What does it mean to you that you are precious to God?

- Do you sense God's heart toward you as he honors you?

2. *God says, "You are forgiven."* We read in Ephesians 1:7: "He is so rich in kindness that he purchased our freedom through the blood of his Son, and our sins are forgiven" (NLT).
   - Take this verse and personalize it: "God is so kind that he has completely forgiven me. I am clean because of the blood of Jesus."
   - What does it mean to you that God has forgiven you?
   - Do you sense God's heart toward you in loving you so much that he purchased your forgiveness with the blood of his only Son?

Take time to thank God for what he has revealed about himself to you. Listen to him as he speaks these words to your heart throughout the coming days and weeks. Let these truths from Scripture work their way deep into your heart and your identity.

CHAPTER 9

Transformation Is a Process

When I trusted Christ as my Savior, my perception of who I am was not transformed automatically. I did not enjoy immediate victory over the deep scars of my past. That was a bit of a disappointment to me.

However, when I trusted Christ, I did receive the Holy Spirit, who has helped heal the old wounds and helped restore my true identity. From that point on it has been a process of growth toward seeing myself through God's eyes and learning to behave accordingly. The positive changes I find in myself today seem almost unbelievable. Still, after all these years, the process continues. It will until I die.

The same is true for you.

When you become a Christian, you become a new person inside. At that point the process of understanding your true identity begins. Paul tells us, "Therefore, if anyone is in Christ, he is a new creation; the old has gone, the new has come!" (2 Cor. 5:17).

If you are like me, you have wished that some of the external things about your past had changed. For example, my childhood with an alcoholic father—and all its memories—did not go away when I became a Christian. You may also have some past experiences that you wish would disappear because they so negatively affected how you look at yourself and life today.

But the newness Paul talked about is spiritual in nature. It describes the internal changes that begin to affect us as we start to grow spiritually in the weeks and months after our conversion. For me, the parents, teachers, peers, and culture that formed my history did not change, but my understanding of those influences gradually changed. Your experience is probably similar. If you had an abusive father growing up, you cannot go back to your childhood and relive it with a loving father. Your past is locked in the past; you can't slip back in time and change it.

PEELING OFF THE GRAVECLOTHES

While the Holy Spirit does the initial transforming work, God chooses to send other believers to help us with the process. The story of how Jesus responded to Lazarus's death illustrates part of the transformation process.

When Jesus approached the tomb of his dead friend Lazarus, he cried out, "Lazarus, come out!" (John 11:43, NLT). On the Master's command, the man who had been dead for four days came alive. Lazarus began a new life.

Lazarus had been wrapped in a linen burial shroud that had been soaked in spices to help preserve the corpse. At Christ's word, new life went right through those graveclothes and into the body, and Lazarus hobbled out of the tomb wrapped up like a mummy.

But, released from the tomb, Lazarus no longer needed his graveclothes. They were definitely an impediment to his activity on the outside. So Jesus told Lazarus's family and friends, "Unwrap him and let him go!" (John 11:44, NLT). With the help of his friends and family, Lazarus was unwrapped and set free to experience his new life.

Notice that the graveclothes did not fall off the moment Christ called out to him. There was a *process* involved in getting Lazarus unwrapped after he had come to life again.

This story paints a picture of what the transformation process is like in our lives. When we become Christians, Christ gives us new life. It is as if he calls to us, "Come out! Come out of your old, dead existence. Come out and enjoy the new life I have prepared for you. Come alive!" Christ is the initiator of the new life. It is his power that activates the transformation process.

But, like Lazarus, we emerge from the tomb of our past shrouded in graveclothes. We may be bound by the negative influences of our family, teachers, or peers. We may be tied up by a faulty self-portrait. Christ's invitation to new life penetrates the graveclothes—the things that bind us—and new life begins, but we are still hobbled by the wrappings. We still need to shed that faulty self-perception and be freed from the negative influences.

The Lord could have chosen to have Lazarus burst out of his graveclothes in a display of power. But he didn't. Christ chose to involve the people in Lazarus's life. He said to Lazarus's friends and family, "You unwrap him! You be part of the process of releasing him from the graveclothes! You help him in the transformation process!" And Christ does the same with us. He continues the process of transformation by bringing into our lives other believers who love us enough to help us see ourselves as God sees us. We will discuss the importance of other believers in the transformation process in chapter 13, "Seeking a Transformational Environment."

DISCOVER WHO YOU ALREADY ARE

Not only is it important for us to remember that transformation is a process begun by the Holy Spirit and assisted by other believers, but it is also essential that we understand another key dynamic: You don't become a new person by changing your behavior; you discover the person you already are in Christ and behave accordingly.

Think about the two parts of that statement for a minute. *You don't become a new person by changing your behavior.* A lot of new

Christians are urged to start *doing* things in order to activate the process of spiritual growth. Well-meaning mentors challenge new converts to study the Bible, memorize verses, attend church as often as possible, witness to others, and replace old, sinful habits with patterns of godly living. Sometimes in our eagerness to see new believers rooted in the faith, we convey that their spiritual activity will transform their spiritual identity.

You don't become a new person by changing your behavior; you discover the person you already are in Christ and behave accordingly.

Don't get me wrong. I am wholeheartedly in favor of Bible study, church attendance, and sharing the faith with others. But studious involvement in these vital activities does not transform us. Think about the last part of the important statement: *You discover the person you already are in Christ and behave accordingly.* Studying the Bible, attending church, and sharing our faith do not cause God to regard us as loved, valued, and competent. He *already* sees us that way because that is who we really are. We don't *do* our way into our identity as God's beloved children; we *are* God's beloved children. When we realize that, we can behave accordingly and do those things that become us.

My friend David Ferguson became a Christian in his early twenties. Well-meaning Christian leaders got him involved in personal Bible study right away to help him start growing in his faith. They loaded him down with materials that challenged him to scrutinize portions of Scripture in order to discover promises to claim, sins to avoid, and commands to obey. It was a very thorough study project, and David dived into it wholeheartedly, spending hours and hours each week digging through the Bible.

But after only a few weeks David was worn out. He was so busy digging out verses in order to "grow" that he had missed the whole point of his exercise. So he set aside the study books and turned his attention to getting to know the God of the Bible personally, the God who had so marvelously saved him. His pursuit led him back into the Word, but his motivation was completely different. Instead of diving into its pages to *become* someone, he scoured the Word to find the heart of the One who had *made* him someone.

We come to see ourselves the way God sees us, through an ongoing, intimate relationship with him.

Today David is one of the most knowledgeable men of the Word I know. More important, he is more intimately in touch with the God of the Word than most Christian leaders. He learned early that Christian growth is primarily a matter of getting to know God in order to see ourselves through his eyes.

We must all be engaged in this process if we are to grasp our true identity. Transforming an inaccurate sense of identity into an increasingly more accurate picture of who we are in Christ comes more from being someone than from doing things. We come to see ourselves the way God sees us, through an ongoing, intimate relationship with him. We read, memorize, and meditate on the Bible primarily to get in touch with God's heart. The more we know God's heart, the more clearly we see that we are lovable, valuable, and competent in his eyes.

GETTING IN TOUCH WITH GOD'S HEART

The truest statements about our identity are found in the Bible. That is where God opens his heart about who we are. If what you think or feel about yourself does not line up with how the Bible describes you, you are living under a case of mistaken identity. The transformation of your inner portrait is inextricably linked to a growing understanding of the Bible's truth about who you are.

Thirty-four-year-old Scott became a Christian in college, but he has lived under a dark cloud of guilt ever since. As a teenager, Scott was involved in a secret homosexual relationship with an older man. After Scott trusted Christ, he changed his lifestyle because he knew that homosexuality is wrong according to Scripture. But Scott could not escape the sense that God still condemned him for his past sin. He felt like a second-class Christian, that God would never trust him with an important ministry because of his teenage mistake. As a result he felt defeated most of the time.

Romans 8:1 declares, "So now there is no condemnation for those who belong to Christ Jesus" (NLT). Who has the accurate picture of Scott's true identity: Scott, who sees himself as condemned and of little value, or God, who has forgiven Scott for his sin and no longer condemns him? God, of course! We see God's heart concerning Scott's sin in Romans 8:1. Scott is forgiven, cleansed. Scott's inaccurate sense of identity began to change only as the truth of Romans 8:1 began to transform how he sees himself.

Apart from the Word of God, we will have great difficulty understanding how God sees us. It is like the man who gave his friend, who loved jigsaw puzzles, an unusual birthday present. The man bought two large puzzles, then switched the box tops on them as a joke. The fellow who received the gift became totally frustrated as he tried to put the first puzzle together. Using the picture on the box top as a guide, he could not make any sense of the pieces inside. He found the second puzzle just as difficult, until his friend revealed the prank.

We experience similar frustration in understanding our identity when we look at the wrong "box top." If you regard your feelings, judgments, and personal experiences as the criteria for determining who you are, you will struggle to "get it together" about your true identity. The Word of God is the picture to go by. The more you are in tune with God's picture, the easier the pieces of your life will fit together to resemble that picture. We must use the true picture of who we are—the Bible—if we hope to experience a needed transformation.

Seeing God for Who He Is

A vital ingredient for seeing ourselves as God sees us is to see God for who he is. The description of God as found in the pages of Scripture reveals his heart to us. The more we know about God, the more we understand why he sees us as loved, valued, and competent.

Consider the following list of characteristics attributed to God in Scripture. Each facet of his character noted here helps us see more clearly why he regards us as he does.[3] You will recognize some of these statements from the journal questions we placed at the end of each chapter in an attempt to help you discover the true heart of the God who loves you.

- God is king of the universe (Ps. 24:8; 1 Chron. 29:11; 2 Chron. 20:6). All your circumstances are ultimately in his hand. He is in control of your life.
- God is righteous (Ps. 119:137). He can only do what is right for you. He cannot sin against you.
- God is just (Deut. 32:4). He will always be fair with you.
- God is love (1 John 4:8). He wants you to get the most out of life.

[3] Adapted from Linda Raney-Wright, *Staying on Top When Things Go Wrong* (Wheaton, Ill.: Tyndale, 1983).

- God is eternal (Deut. 33:27). His plan for your life transcends time into eternity.
- God is all-knowing (2 Chron. 16:9; Ps. 139:1-6). He knows all about you, past and present, and he knows how to bring good out of even your worst experiences.
- God is everywhere (Ps. 139:7-10). There is no place you can go that he cannot take care of you.
- God is all-powerful (Job 42:2). God can do anything necessary to accomplish his purpose in your life.
- God is truth (Ps. 31:5). He cannot lie to you.
- God is unchangeable (Mal. 3:6). He is not fickle or moody. You can depend on him.
- God is faithful (Ps. 33:4; Exod. 34:6). You can trust him to do what he says.
- God is holy (Rev. 15:4). Everything he does in your life will be in harmony with his holy character.

Seeing Yourself As God Sees You

The Bible also reveals to us what God says about who you are. It reveals his heart about you. The elements of your identity listed in the rest of this chapter were true of you from the moment you trusted Christ as Savior and Lord. "We have all been baptized into Christ's body by one Spirit, and we have all received the same Spirit" (1 Cor. 12:13, NLT). At the moment of salvation, all of us were baptized into Christ, providing the foundation of our new identity.

The first two chapters of the epistle to the Ephesians contain a concentrated dose of your true identity as a new creation in Christ. The passages below describe our position in Christ. Please note: These statements from God's Word are *already* true of you because you are in Christ. They are part of your identity apart from your performance as a believer. I have related them in the first person so you can reread this list often to help you see yourself clearly as God sees you.

- I am blessed in the heavenly realm with every spiritual blessing in Christ (1:3).
- I was chosen before the creation of the world to be holy and blameless in God's sight (1:4).
- I was predestined to be adopted as his child through Jesus Christ (1:5).
- I have redemption through his blood (1:7).
- I am forgiven (1:7).
- I am sealed in Christ with the Holy Spirit (1:13).

Because of our position in Christ, great things are true of us, truth Paul wants us to internalize. He therefore prays that "the eyes of your heart may be enlightened in order that you may know the hope to which he has called you, the riches of his glorious inheritance in the saints, and his incomparably great power for us who believe" (Eph. 1:18-19). God is deeply concerned that we see ourselves as he sees us.

Paul goes on to describe Christ's resurrection and ascension to the right hand of the Father (see 1:20-23). He adds that we were raised with Christ and seated with him next to the Father (see Eph. 2:6). Then in chapter 2 he continues with more descriptions of the believer as seen from God's perspective. Again, I have paraphrased these statements in the first person.

- I am alive together with Christ (2:5).
- I am raised up with Christ (2:6).
- I am seated with Christ in the heavenly realms (2:6).
- I am saved by his grace (2:8).
- I am God's workmanship (2:10).
- I have direct access to God through the Spirit (2:18).

117

In addition to this concentrated dose in Ephesians 1 and 2, God's Word abounds with descriptions of how God sees us. Here is another list of statements that reflect your true identity. Read these statements aloud to yourself as often as possible. Meditate on these truths during the week so that God can use them to shine the spotlight on your true self-portrait.[4]

- I have peace with God (Rom. 5:1).
- I am a child of God (John 1:12).
- I am indwelled by the Holy Spirit (1 Cor. 3:16).
- I have access to God's wisdom (James 1:5).
- I am helped by God (Heb. 4:16).
- I am reconciled to God (Rom. 5:11).
- I am not condemned by God (Rom. 8:1).
- I am justified (Rom. 5:1).
- I have Christ's righteousness (Rom. 5:19; 2 Cor. 5:21).
- I am his ambassador (2 Cor. 5:20).
- I am completely forgiven (Col. 1:14).
- I am tenderly loved by God (Jer. 31:3).
- I am the sweet fragrance of Christ to God (2 Cor. 2:15).
- I am a temple in which God dwells (1 Cor. 3:16).
- I am blameless and beyond reproach (Col. 1:22).
- I am the salt of the earth (Matt. 5:13).
- I am the light of the world (Matt. 5:14).
- I am a branch on Christ's vine (John 15:1, 5).
- I am Christ's friend (John 15:15).
- I am chosen by Christ to bear fruit (John 15:16).
- I am a joint heir with Christ, sharing his inheritance with him (Rom. 8:17).
- I am united to the Lord, one spirit with him (1 Cor. 6:17).
- I am a member of Christ's body (1 Cor. 12:27).

[4]Part of this list is adapted from Neil T. Anderson, *Victory Over the Darkness* (Regal Books, 1990), 45-47, 57-59.

- I am a saint (Eph. 1:1).
- I am hidden with Christ in God (Col. 3:3).
- I am chosen by God, holy and dearly loved (Col. 3:12).
- I am a child of the light (1 Thess. 5:5).
- I am a holy partaker of God's heavenly calling (Heb. 3:1).
- I am sanctified (Heb. 2:11).
- I am one of God's living stones, being built up in Christ as a spiritual house (1 Pet. 2:5).
- I am a member of a chosen race, a royal priesthood, a holy nation, a people for God's own possession (1 Pet. 2:9-10).
- I am firmly rooted and built up in Christ (Col. 2:7).
- I am born of God, and the evil one cannot touch me (1 John 5:18).
- I have the mind of Christ (1 Cor. 2:16).
- I may approach God with boldness, freedom, and confidence (Eph. 3:12).
- I have been rescued from Satan's domain and transferred into the kingdom of Christ (Col. 1:13).
- I have been made complete in Christ (Col. 2:10).
- I have been given a spirit of power, love, and self-discipline (2 Tim. 1:7).
- I have been given great and precious promises by God (2 Pet. 1:4).
- My needs are met by God (Phil. 4:19).

Are you beginning to see more clearly what Paul meant by his statement that you are a new creation in Christ? One of the keys to the transformation of your sense of identity is to acknowledge that something very good happened to you when you trusted Christ. In Paul's words, you have "put on the new self, which is being renewed in knowledge in the image of its Creator" (Col. 3:10).

You are not primarily what your parents, teachers, or friends say you are, even though many of them may be Christians. You are not primarily the product of your religious experiences, even though many of them may have been positive. And you are certainly not what the godless culture says you are. You are who God says you are—nothing more, nothing less. The more you review, recite, and internalize the verbal picture God paints of you in Scripture, the more you will grow like that picture.

> *You are who God says you are—
> nothing more, nothing less.*

In the next three chapters, we will look specifically at how a growing, experiential knowledge of God the Father, Jesus Christ the Son, and the Holy Spirit contributes to the transformation of your inner portrait.

GETTING A CLEARER PICTURE OF YOUR IDENTITY
Part of understanding who you are involves understanding who God is and experiencing his heart toward you. Reflect on the following truths about God. Take time to write your responses to the questions in a notebook or journal.

1. *God is your security.* We read in Deuteronomy 33:12: "Let the beloved of the Lord rest secure in him, for he shields him all day long, and the one the Lord loves rests between his shoulders."
   • What does it mean to you that God loves you and makes it safe for you to rest in him?

- What does it mean to you that God allows you to rest between his shoulders?

2. *God is unchanging.* We read in Psalm 102:27: "You are always the same" (NLT).
   - What does it mean to you that God is always the same, always predictable?
   - What does it mean to you that the God who found you lovable when he created you finds you lovable, valuable, and competent today?

A second part of understanding who you are involves hearing what God says about who *you* are. Listen to God's voice speaking to you:

1. *God says, "You are blameless."* We read in Colossians 1:22: "You are holy and blameless as you stand before him without a single fault" (NLT).
   - Take this verse and personalize it: "Because Jesus died for me, I am blameless and can stand before God without a single fault."
   - What does it mean to you that God finds you so valuable that he would allow his perfect Son to die so that you can see yourself as blameless?
   - Do you sense God's heart toward you in making you clean?

2. *God says, "You are rescued from darkness and brought into God's kingdom."* We read in Colossians 1:13: "He has rescued us from the one who rules in the kingdom of darkness, and he has brought us into the Kingdom of his dear Son" (NLT).
   - Take this verse and personalize it: "God loved me enough to rescue me from the kingdom of darkness and to bring me into his dear Son's kingdom."

- What does it mean to you that God rescued you from darkness?
- Do you sense God's heart toward you in bringing you into the kingdom of his precious Son?

Take time to thank God for what he has revealed about himself to you. Listen to him as he speaks these words to your heart throughout the coming days and weeks. Let these truths from Scripture work their way deep into your heart and your identity.

FOUR

Aligning Your Perception with God's Perception

CHAPTER 10

A New Sense of Being Loved

Your personal relationship with God is the gateway to understanding your true identity. In relating to God the Father, your sense of belonging grows, and you understand that you are unconditionally loved by God. In relating to Jesus Christ the Son, your sense of worth grows, and you understand that you are valued by God. In relating to the Holy Spirit, your sense of competence grows, and you understand that you are useful to God. These three pillars are the foundation to your identity as God's loved, valued, competent child. In the next three chapters we will explore each of them in greater detail.

LOVE THAT TOUCHES THE HEART

Our most basic human need is to be loved and to sense that we belong to someone. You may know intellectually that you are loved. After all, the Bible declares God's love for us. And someone very close to you—a parent, boyfriend or girlfriend, spouse, child, or dear friend—has probably spoken those magical words, "I love you." But hearing about being loved is not enough. Do you know what it *feels* like to be loved? Only when your comprehension of love encompasses the intellect *and* the emotions do you experience the sense that you belong.

Consider the list of scriptural statements in the last chapter. As you read those statements about who you are because of what God has done, what does it do to your heart? For example, you know that God loves you because John 1:12 declares that when you received Christ, you became a child of God. You may be able to exegete that passage from the original Greek and explain every nuance of every word. *Knowing* the verse inside and out may be helpful, but such knowledge does not mean you have *experienced* God's love. Rather, how does it make you feel to know that the God who created the universe desires a close, family relationship with you? What emotions are aroused when you realize that the One who exists from eternity to eternity desires to call you his son or daughter and invites you to call him "Abba, Father" (Rom. 8:15)?

God does not need you to complete his life or meet his needs in any way. Your step of faith in Christ did not force God to do something he did not want to do. He loves you because he chooses to. He welcomes you into his arms as a dearly loved child simply because he wants you as his child. What does that reality do for you emotionally?

I'll tell you what it does for me. I feel very humbled, special, and cared for. "You choose me?" I respond to God in amazement. "You know all about me, my past, present, and future sin, my weaknesses, my faithlessness, my lack of love at times, and you still want me as your child? It's too good to be true, and yet you are God, so it *is* true!" The more I sense God's love by allowing it to grip my heart, the deeper my sense of belonging. As God meets this core need in my life, I see myself differently.

Contrast this emotional impact with other expressions of so-called love in your life. You may have grown up in a home where people said they loved you or where love was implied because a parent figure provided food and shelter for you. But did love go beyond words and perfunctory deeds to convey the sense that you were lovable, that you were wanted, that you belonged? Did the love that was supposed to be in your home touch your heart deeply?

126

Recently Dottie and I attended a conference hosted by David and Teresa Ferguson. Among the other conference attendees were Carla and her husband. During one small-group discussion on the topic of family background, Carla described her relationship with her mother and father as average. But as David and Teresa lovingly probed with questions, Carla's responses painted a different picture.

Carla mentioned that her mother rarely listened to her as a child. She would come home from school with excited news, but Mom was often too busy preparing the family dinner to pay attention to such childish chatter. Riding in the car together, Carla would try to make conversation, but her mother showed little interest in Carla's activities, either by not listening or by dominating the conversation with her own agenda. To this day, Carla concluded, mother-daughter conversations are dominated by her mother's needs. It has been largely a one-way relationship throughout most of Carla's life.

David astutely observed that Carla's relationship with her mother should be categorized as distant rather than average. Carla's mother would insist that she loves her daughter dearly. But because of the mother's self-centeredness and inattention, especially during Carla's childhood, Carla missed out on a large measure of belonging at home, which subtly conveyed to her that she was not entirely lovable.

As the discussion continued, Carla tearfully revealed that her father, a hard-working provider, had fondled her inappropriately as a child. Teresa gently corrected Carla; her relationship with her father was not average but abusive. A loving father gives to meet his child's needs; Carla's father had wrongly taken from her to meet his own needs. It was another reason why Carla's relationship with seemingly good parents had left her wanting for love and belonging at home.

Perhaps you arrived at adulthood with a similar inner ache. Your parents or guardians provided for your physical needs adequately, but they failed to give of themselves to the point that their love gripped your heart with a sense that you were deeply loved and wanted. As a result you struggle to accept the reality that you are lovable, that you belong. In order to transform your sense of identity, you need to shore up this vital first pillar of who you are.

THE ONE WHO KNOWS YOU BEST LOVES YOU MOST

The most significant aspect of God's thoughts and feelings toward you is his unconditional love and acceptance. The apostle John, who called himself "the disciple whom Jesus loved" (John 13:23), wrote, "This is real love. It is not that we loved God, but that he loved us and sent his Son as a sacrifice to take away our sins" (1 John 4:10, NLT). Nothing about you caused God to love you; he just does!

Nothing about you caused God to love you; he just does!

This is where the transformation begins. Too often we lose sight of the truth that God loves us—period. Before you trusted Christ, God loved you as much as he loves you now (see Rom. 5:8; 8:38-39). Jesus pointed out the extent of this love when he said, "As the Father has loved me, so have I loved you. Now remain in my love" (John 15:9). It is staggering to think that Christ loves us as much as the Father loves him. Such love is difficult to grasp intellectually, let alone to experience emotionally.

Many people today find it difficult to receive unconditional love from God and others because the love they received growing up was conditional. The expression "I love you" was always attached to an "if" or a "because." This was Rick's experience. Rick, a believer, was visiting his Christian friend Bart. During the visit,

Bart put his hand on Rick's shoulder and said, "I don't know if I have ever told you this, but I really love you, Rick." It was a simple, heartfelt expression of Bart's unconditional love for his friend.

Instead of receiving the warm expression, Rick snapped, "What do you want?" Perplexed, Bart answered, "I don't want anything. What are you talking about?"

Rick did not reply, and soon after the exchange, he went home. Later, he returned to Bart's home to ask his forgiveness for his unkind response. "I'm not used to someone loving me without wanting something from me," he explained. "My parents told me they loved me only when they wanted me to get better grades or change my behavior in some way."

Some people respond to God the same way Rick responded to Bart: "What do you want?" Such a response generally means that unconditional love was rarely experienced during a person's formative years. God's love is not offered to us with strings attached. Yes, he desires our loving and obedient response to him. But he loves us whether or not we fulfill that desire.

Other people feel the need to bargain with God over receiving unconditional love from him, rationalizing, "I need to straighten out my life before you can accept me as I am." God responds, "I already accept you just the way you are. I proved it by sending my Son to die for you while you were lost in your sin" (see Rom. 5:8).

There are no grounds in Scripture for the argument that we must perform at a certain level before God can accept us. Paul wrote, "It is by grace you have been saved, through faith—and this not from yourselves, it is the gift of God—not by works, so that no one can boast" (Eph. 2:8-9). Our acceptance with God is not based on our good deeds or attitudes or on anything we have done for him. He loves us unconditionally because of what *he* has done. His work becomes personal for us when we place our trust in Christ and accept him as Savior and Lord. Scripture declares, "To all who received him, to those who believed in his name, he gave the right to become children of God" (John 1:12).

God always expects the best of us, always expects that we will succeed. Yet even when we fail, we do not jeopardize our acceptance with him. He does not lecture us unkindly. He never says, "I told you so." He allows the consequences of our mistakes to teach us, and he applies loving discipline when we sin. But he accepts us where we are and works with us and through us to promote our growth, even though he already knows we will fall short again and again.

Our acceptance with God is not based on our good deeds or attitudes or on anything we have done for him.

LOVED AND ACCEPTED EVEN WHEN HEADED THE WRONG WAY

A famous story from the annals of the Rose Bowl illustrates what it means to have someone believe in you and accept you unconditionally.

In 1929, a University of California football player, Roy Riegels, made Rose Bowl history. In the second quarter of the game, he scooped up a Georgia Tech fumble and headed for the end zone—the *wrong* end zone. He was tackled by a teammate just before crossing the goal line. Riegels's mistake would have earned Georgia Tech six points.

Riegels's team had to punt from their own end zone. Georgia Tech blocked the kick, resulting in a two-point safety, the margin that eventually won the game for Georgia Tech.

During half-time, the California players filed glumly to the dressing room. Riegels slumped in a corner, buried his face in his hands, and cried uncontrollably. Coach Price offered no half-time pep talk. What could he say? As the team got ready to go out for the second half, his only comment was, "Men, the same team that played the first half will start the second."

The players started for the door, all but Roy Riegels. Coach Price walked to the corner where Riegels sat and said quietly, "Roy, didn't you hear me?" Then he repeated the instructions he had given to the team.

"Coach, I can't do it," Roy said dejectedly. "I have ruined you, the university, and myself. I can't face that crowd again to save my life."

Coach Price put his hand on his player's shoulder. "Roy, get up and go back; the game is only half over." Inspired by his coach's confidence, Roy Riegels went out to play again. After the game, the Georgia Tech players commented that Riegels played harder in the second half than they had ever seen anyone else play.

We find in Coach Price a glimmer of God's accepting attitude toward us. We make mistakes. We occasionally run in the wrong direction. We stumble and fall and shrink from God in shame. But he comes to us and says, "Get up and keep going; the game is only half over." That's unconditional love. As you receive and enjoy God's unconditional love, you will see more clearly that you are unconditionally lovable!

Think for a moment about what happened to you when you trusted Christ as your Savior and when God accepted you as his child. You were born again (see John 3:3-5; 1 Pet. 1:23). You became an heir of God (see Eph. 1:13-14; Rom. 8:17). You were adopted into God's family (see Eph. 1:5). God poured his love into your heart (see Rom. 5:5). You became one with Christ in such a way that you will never be parted from him (see John 17:23; Gal. 2:20; Heb. 13:5). Nothing will ever separate you from God's love (see Rom. 8:38-39). You will spend eternity with God in a place he has prepared for you (see John 14:1-4). You were welcomed into a new family, and you are a member in good standing throughout eternity (see 1 Cor. 12:13, 27).

In light of all God has done to prove his unconditional love, what prevents you from regarding yourself as lovable? If God loves you, you must be lovable. The fact that God loves you unconditionally in spite of your flaws and failures should continue to motivate you to accept yourself.

If you cannot accept yourself the way you are—limitations as well as assets, weaknesses as well as strengths, shortcomings as well as abilities—you will have difficulty allowing anyone else to accept you as you are. You will always put up a front to prevent people from knowing what you are really like. And it is even harder to live the life of a phony than to live transparently, even when it means others sometimes see you at your worst. One of the greatest needs of the church today is for Christians to live out the scriptural admonition, "Accept one another . . . just as Christ accepted you, in order to bring praise to God" (Rom. 15:7). We can fulfill this admonition only when we see ourselves as God sees us: completely lovable.

LIFE IN THE FAMILY

If anyone is able to enjoy a sense of belonging, it is the child of God. You belong to God and his family. The apostle John wrote, "How great is the love the Father has lavished on us, that we should be called children of God! And that is what we are!" (1 John 3:1). As soon as John wrote the words "children of God," he must have paused to let that truth sink in because he concludes the thought with an exclamation. If John were here today, he might say it this way: "Wow, we really *are* children of God! That's incredible!"

Some Christians may argue, "But we are only *adopted* children in God's family." Somehow the fact that God adopted us causes them to feel like second-class heirs.

I have been impressed with how one father, my longtime friend Dick Day, views adoption. After having had the experience of parenting their five biological children, Dick and his wife, Charlotte, went to Korea and adopted Jimmy. Dick says, "That little guy Jimmy is my son. He has the same rights and privileges as our other five children. He has the same access to our inheritance, our time, and our love."

Dick's statement raised my level of appreciation for the place we occupy in God's family. God has adopted us, but he has declared us "heirs of God and co-heirs with Christ" (Rom. 8:17). That means we share equally in Christ's inheritance. God sees us just as my friend Dick sees Jimmy.

Has this truth dawned on you in force? Have you uttered that exclamation with enlightened wonder: "Wow, I really am a child of God! I really belong"? This biblical insight is a key to the transformation of your sense of identity.

No Longer An Island

The Father obviously knew that we would struggle at times not only with grasping the reality of being lovable to him and others but also with sensing that we belong. So he built into his plan for us a support system. God established the church as a place where love and acceptance may be continually modeled and experienced. He gave us the church as a tangible expression of the eternal reality that we belong. Fellowship and interaction with other believers is indispensable to the transformation of your sense of who you are.

As Jesus prepared to die and return to heaven, he proclaimed, "Believe me when I say that I am in the Father and the Father is in me" (John 14:11). Two persons are mentioned in this union: God the Father and God the Son. The next few verses talk about God sending a third person, the Holy Spirit. And then Christ said, "On that day [perhaps referring to Pentecost and the birth of the church] you will realize that I am in my Father, and you are in me, and I am in you" (v. 20).

What did Jesus mean when he said, "I am in my Father, and you are in me, and I am in you"? When you believed in Christ as your Savior and Lord, you were placed into Christ and Christ took up his residence in you. And since Jesus and his Father are in union, you are also in the Father and the Father is in you. Talk about a sense of belonging!

God established the church as a place where love and acceptance may be continually modeled and experienced.

But there is more. If the Father is in me and you, and if we are both in the Father, you and I have a very special, close relationship. I might even say that, because of our mutual, intimate relationship with God, I am in you and you are in me. As a Christian, you are not an island; you are a peninsula, and so am I. We are both integrally involved in the body of Christ, and thus we are vitally involved with each other.

You and I are just two of the living members mentioned in 1 Corinthians 12: "For we were all baptized by one Spirit into one body . . . and we were all given the one Spirit to drink. . . . But God has combined the members of the body and has given greater honor to the parts that lacked it, so that there should be no division in the body, but that its parts should have equal concern for each other. If one part suffers, every part suffers with it; if one part is honored, every part rejoices with it. Now you are the body of Christ, and each one of you is a part of it" (1 Cor. 12:13, 24-27).

Notice what Paul concludes about our vital relationship. There is to be no division between us, and we are to have equal concern for one another. That means that since God sees you as lovable, I must do everything in my power to affirm that you are lovable. This is what the church is all about. That is why it is so important for you to be involved in ongoing fellowship with a group of believers. We cannot show equal concern for one another if we are not together on a consistent basis.

In a sense, every believer plays the dual role of Coach Price and Roy Riegels in the church. When you fumble or fail, someone in your church or Bible study group is there to remind you that you are loved and accepted despite your mistakes. And when someone in your group goes the wrong way and feels ashamed, you get to come along like Coach Price with encouraging words. Such mutual caring is a practical expression of Paul's admonition, "Encourage one another and build each other up" (1 Thess. 5:11).

What is the end result of this mutual, heartfelt caring? First, biblical love and acceptance are not just *understood*, they are *experienced*. This is the way love grips the heart. Second, as objects of affirmation and encouragement, believers gain a clearer picture of how God sees them. Think about it: If those closest to you in the faith are constantly reminding you that they love you and that God loves you, you are more likely to get the clue that you are lovable. Third, the constant affirmation of love and acceptance helps resolve hurts from the past. When we begin to love people as God loves them, sad experiences of being unloved in the past can be healed.

A friend of mine used a clever code message with his children while they were growing up. Whenever he signed a birthday card for them or left them a note or sent them a postcard from a trip, he added the seven letters J. L. Y. A. S. D. I. Sometimes when he was with his children around other people, he would say the letters, conveying the message they knew well as if it was their special secret. The letters stood for "Jesus loves you and so do I." Every time the kids saw or heard the letters, they were reminded that their dad's love for them was linked to God's love.

That's the way you begin to transform a distorted sense of identity into God's exquisite picture of you. Plant yourself in a group of loving believers, and let God's unconditional love touch you through them.

GETTING A CLEARER PICTURE OF YOUR IDENTITY

Part of understanding who you are involves understanding who God is and experiencing his heart toward you. Reflect on the following truths about God. Take time to write your responses to the questions in a notebook or journal.

> 1. *God is loving.* We read in Mark 10:16: "Then he took the children into his arms and placed his hands on their heads and blessed them" (NLT).
> - What does it mean to you that God takes you in his arms and blesses you?
> - What does it mean to you that a loving God finds you lovable?
>
> 2. *God is your protector.* We read in Deuteronomy 33:27: "The eternal God is your refuge, and his everlasting arms are under you" (NLT).
> - What does it mean to you that God's arms are everlastingly under and around you?
> - What does it mean to you that because God loves you, he will protect you?

A second part of understanding who you are involves hearing what God says about who *you* are. Listen to God's voice speaking to you:

1. *God says, "You are deeply loved by me."* We read in
   Daniel 10:19: "Don't be afraid," he said, "for you are
   deeply loved by God" (NLT).
   - Take this verse and personalize it: "God loves me
     deeply. As a result, I do not have to be afraid or inse-
     cure. I can see myself as lovable."
   - What does it mean to you that God loves you deeply
     and eternally?
   - Do you sense God's heart toward you in surrounding
     you with his unchanging love?

2. *God says, "You belong to me; you are mine."* We read in
   Isaiah 43:1: "I have called you by name; you are mine"
   (NLT).
   - Take this verse and personalize it: "The God of the
     universe has called me by name. He says I belong to
     him."
   - What does it mean to you that you belong to God?
   - Do you sense God's heart toward you in calling you
     by name and giving you a place to belong?

Take time to thank God for what he has revealed about himself to
you. Listen to him as he speaks these words to your heart throughout the coming days and weeks. Let these truths from Scripture
work their way deep into your heart and your identity.

CHAPTER 11

A New Sense of Worth

Several centuries ago, a Protestant scholar named Morena was forced into exile in Lombardy, Italy. Living in poverty, Morena fell seriously ill and was taken to a paupers' hospital. The physicians, assuming that the wretched-looking patient was uneducated, began conversing in Latin among themselves at his bedside. They said, "This worthless creature is going to die anyway, so let us try an experiment on him."

Morena, of course, knew Latin almost as well as his native language. Summoning his strength, he raised himself up and said to the surprised physicians, "How can you call 'worthless' someone for whom Jesus died?"

In our society, a person's value is determined in many different ways. A Major League Baseball team may consider one player worth tens of millions of dollars over his playing career. A soldier in combat may discover that he is worth a human life when a comrade takes a bullet to save him. A single mother on welfare may find that she is worth the time and effort of a group of volunteers who spend days repairing and painting her dilapidated house.

As Morena clearly understood, our principal value as Christians derives from the fact that God the Father allowed Jesus Christ—his sinless Son—to die for our sins. The apostle Peter remarked that money pales in comparison to such a sacrifice: "For

139

you know that God paid a ransom to save you from the empty life you inherited from your ancestors. And the ransom he paid was not mere gold or silver. He paid for you with the precious lifeblood of Christ, the sinless, spotless Lamb of God" (1 Pet. 1:18-19, NLT).

Jesus declared the high value of giving one's life for another when he said, "Greater love has no one than this, that he lay down his life for his friends" (John 15:13). Paul expanded on that thought to describe the ultimate life-for-life sacrifice: "Now, no one is likely to die for a good person, though someone might be willing to die for a person who is especially good. But God showed his great love for us by sending Christ to die for us while we were still sinners" (Rom. 5:7-8, NLT).

In God's estimation, we were worth the death of his Son. We had nothing to attract God to us or to provoke him to send his Son to die for us. We were not righteous or moral; we were still sinners, the very antithesis of the perfect Lamb. But God saw us as lovable, and our value rose astronomically when Jesus gave up his life for us. No matter what your value may be to others in earthly terms, you are eternally priceless because of the ransom the Father lovingly paid for you.

IF YOU WERE THE ONLY PERSON ON EARTH

Sometimes it is easy for individual Christians to feel lost in the crowd. We may say, "Sure, Jesus died for my sins, but he didn't die for me alone. He died for the whole world. I'm just one among multiplied millions of people who received God's gift of forgiveness in his salvation 'group plan.'"

The fact that you are only one redeemed believer among millions in no way diminishes the personal nature of your value to God. If you and your family were the only persons on earth, do you believe Christ would have died for you? Absolutely! God's first promise to redeem fallen mankind was issued when there was only one couple on earth. After Adam and Eve sinned, God promised to crush Satan's head, referring to Christ's victory over sin on the cross (see Gen. 3:15). If you had been there in the Garden of Eden instead of Adam and Eve, you also would have disobeyed God, and the promise would have been made concerning you.

You must catch a fresh vision of your worthiness to God in order to transform your sense of identity to line up with how God sees you. Since you belong to God and his family, you are worthy to receive "the manifold grace of God" (1 Pet. 4:10, KJV). This picture is often missing when we talk about Christ's work at Calvary. Ask the average believer what Calvary was all about, and he or she will likely say, "It was about sin and forgiveness." But we must look a little closer. *Why* did God deal with our sin and offer forgiveness at Calvary? Because we are lovable to him, and the only way we could belong to his family was if Christ died for our sin. Because we are lovable to him, we are worth the death of his Son. As you perceive your value to God more clearly, it will affect how you live and interact with others.

Once again, it is not enough simply to *know* that you are valuable to God. This truth must also grip your heart to the point that you *feel* valued. I hope that this chapter will expand both your mind and your emotions on the topic of your worth to God.

YOU ARE WORTH GOD'S ATTENTION

When you were a child, who got down on the floor and played blocks or dolls or soldiers with you? Which adults in your life periodically left the world of their jobs and responsibilities and entered your world of toys, games, and "pretend"? I hope that there were several: your parents, grandparents, aunts and uncles, older siblings or cousins, family friends. A child's need for attention is met when a loving adult leaves the grown-up world for a period of time and enters the child's world.

Sadly, many children grow up without this need being met, especially by their dad or mom. A parent figure is often too busy to be interested and involved in the child's world. Or a parent spends time with the child by calling him or her into the parent's world. For example, Dad considers it quality father-son time when his three-year-old boy, who cares little about sports, sits next to him while he watches a baseball game on television. Children who grow up without attention perceive themselves as unworthy of an adult's time and involvement.

You may have grown up in a home where you received very little genuine attention from the adults who should have loved you in this way. As a result, you may regard yourself as being of questionable value to God and others. Put another way, your inner portrait may be marked with a "bargain basement discount" tag. You may see yourself as less than first quality because significant people in your life failed to meet your need for attention.

Allow your heart to be gripped with the reality of your value to God, who met your need for attention in the fullest sense. God left his world—heaven—in the person of Jesus Christ and entered your world—sinful earth—to declare your worthiness as the object of his love. Paul wrote, "Christ Jesus . . . being in very nature God, did not consider equality with God something to be grasped, but made himself nothing, taking the very nature of a servant, being made in human likeness. And being found in appearance as a man, he humbled himself and became obedient to death—even death on a cross!" (Phil. 2:5-8).

Furthermore, God values you so highly that he remains in your world day by day in the person of his Spirit (see John 14:16; Matt. 28:20). He knows every detail about you since before you were born (see Ps. 139:13-16). He is keenly attentive to the troubles that plague you daily, inviting you to "give all your worries and cares to God, for he cares about what happens to you" (1 Pet. 5:7, NLT). He is intimately involved in your moment-by-moment existence on this earth because he is here with you. No wonder one of Christ's names is " 'Immanuel'—which means, 'God with us' " (Matt. 1:23).

What kind of emotions are stirred within you when you consider that Christ left the glory of heaven to meet your deepest needs? How valued do you feel knowing that Christ will bear in his glorified body for eternity the scars of your redemption, perpetual reminders that he loved you enough to enter your world? How does your heart respond to the awareness that God sees you as valuable and worthy? As you allow this truth to flood your mind and heart, you will experience a transformation in how you see yourself.

Once again, the body of Christ plays an indispensable role in your transformation. Are you intimately involved with at least a small group of believers who reflect God's perception of your value? Are there a few Christians who love you enough to enter your world and care about your work, your spiritual growth, your struggles, and even your hobbies and interests? Similarly, are you growing to value your fellow believers as God does? Do you emulate God's attentiveness by leaving your world when necessary to demonstrate that you love and value your fellow believers? Cultivating and maintaining an environment of worthiness in human relationships gives us a clearer view of how God sees us.

YOU ARE WORTH GOD'S FORGIVENESS

Do you find it hard to believe that God continues to forgive you daily for your sins? All of us are quick to agree with the Christian confession that states that we sin in thought, word, and deed every day. But are we just as quick to agree that "if we confess our sins, he is faithful and just and will forgive us our sins and purify us from all unrighteousness" (1 John 1:9)—even though we must do so day after day? If you find it difficult to accept God's limitless forgiveness, you have a problem with your sense of what you mean to God. You have established an arbitrary limit on your value to God. In effect, you are unable to see yourself as worthy of God's forgiving you. This perception probably stems from the fact that you were not always forgiven for your mistakes as a child.

Hebrews 10:12 states, "When this priest [Christ] had offered for all time one sacrifice for sins, he sat down at the right hand of God." The effects of this once-and-for-all sacrifice for sin are seen in Colossians 2:13-14: "He forgave all our sins. He canceled the record that contained the charges against us. He took it and destroyed it by nailing it to Christ's cross" (NLT). King David was guilty of adultery and murder, and yet he could say, "Then I acknowledged my sin to you and did not cover up my iniquity. I said, 'I will confess my transgressions to the Lord'—and you forgave the guilt of my sin" (Ps. 32:5). What freedom to see ourselves as God sees us: forgiven of all our sins—past, present, and future.

Yet some Christians are convinced that they have sinned too much, too long, or too greatly to be forgiven. They believe that God forgives, but they wrongly assess that they have used up the amount of forgiveness God has allotted to them. A seventeen-year-old student, whom I will call Cindy, expressed her sad state to me in a letter:

> Josh, I'm writing to you because I'm alone and confused. I had sex with my boyfriend, thinking I owed it to him. About four months later I learned I was pregnant. Jeff left me, and my parents still don't know. About a month ago I became a Christian. But I have been feeling so guilty. How can God love me after what I have done? I feel that my life is not worth living any more. I cry myself to sleep every night. I sometimes wish I were dead. My parents and I don't get along too well. They have been Christians all their lives, and they wouldn't understand what I'm going through. I'm just so confused. Can God really love me and forgive me? Please write back.

Cindy does not yet realize her great value to God. When Jesus left his world and died for her sins, he paid for *all* of them, including the improper sexual relationship that left her pregnant and despondent. Yet Cindy thinks her sin is too great, like a check that has bounced because of insufficient funds in the account to cover it. She needs to see that she cannot exhaust God's account of forgiveness. He placed no limits on forgiveness. Every sin we confess, he forgives. And that is what I told Cindy in my letter of response.

A good illustration of the extent of God's forgiveness is the life of King Manasseh, one of Judah's most wicked kings. Manasseh turned his back on God, worshiped false gods, and led the people in idolatry (see 2 Chron. 33:1-9). If Cindy thought it impossible for God to forgive her, she would have to believe that God could not forgive Manasseh because he was so evil.

However, when the Assyrians captured the nation of Judah and its king, Manasseh "sought the favor of the Lord his God and humbled himself greatly before the God of his fathers. And when he prayed to him, the Lord was moved by his entreaty and listened to his plea; so he brought him back to Jerusalem and to his kingdom. Then Manasseh knew that the Lord is God" (2 Chron. 33:12-13). Despite Manasseh's evil past, God compassionately forgave him. I believe that the forgiven king returned to his homeland able to see himself more as God saw him, worthy of being forgiven.

Like Cindy, a lot of Christians see themselves as beyond forgiveness. But how does God see us? King David, who did not consider himself beyond forgiveness, wrote, "[The Lord] does not treat us as our sins deserve or repay us according to our iniquities. For as high as the heavens are above the earth, so great is his love for those who fear him; as far as the east is from the west, so far has he removed our transgressions from us" (Ps. 103:10-12). In the shadow of his sin and remorse, David saw clearly God's unlimited forgiveness that established in him a sense of worthiness.

Letting Yourself Off the Hook

Another exciting aspect of God's forgiveness is that we are free to forgive ourselves. Many Christians I talk to accept God's forgiveness, but they cannot forgive themselves. They are harder on themselves than God is! If God values us enough to pay for our sins and forgive us, who are we to say we are not worthy of forgiveness? Transforming our sense of identity means letting ourselves off the hook and accepting the forgiveness God provides.

Several years ago while eating at a restaurant with some friends, I said something I never should have said. I hurt a brother in Christ deeply with my words. On the way home, I realized the impact of my uncalled-for, off-the-wall remark. I returned to the restaurant immediately to make it right. I acknowledged to my friend that what I had done was a sin, and I asked his forgiveness. He looked me squarely in the eye and said, "I will not forgive you. Someone in your position should never have said that."

Taken aback by his surprising response, I said, "I know I never should have said it; that's why I am asking your forgiveness." I did everything I could to make things right, but my brother was determined not to forgive me.

I went home feeling frustrated and confused. I began to struggle spiritually and emotionally over the situation. Feeling extremely guilty, I began to berate myself mentally. *How could you have said that, Josh?* My false guilt drew me into thoughts of self-condemnation. *How can you be in Christian work and hurt a brother like that? How can God use you in ministry when you speak to people that way?* I was full of self-pity and the misery of personal guilt.

Then the Holy Spirit began to work on my thinking. I replayed the entire incident in my mind, including my response, in light of Scripture and my relationship with Christ. I thought, *Josh, you're not handling this correctly. You can make one of two responses in this situation. One, you can continue to feel sorry for yourself, wallow in guilt, and focus on your own frailty and sin. Two, you can realize that*

Jesus died for this situation, confess your sin to God, accept God's forgiveness, and do all you can to make it right with your brother. Having done all you can do, forgive yourself, lift your head and square your shoulders, and resume walking by faith.

After wrestling with the alternatives a short while, I chose to acknowledge God's forgiveness, forgive myself, continue to walk by faith, and do everything I could do to heal the relationship with a wounded, unforgiving brother.

If you choose not to forgive yourself, be aware that you are not seeing yourself as God sees you.

At that moment I was deeply aware that forgiving myself was not dependent on the forgiveness of my offended brother, even though God did expect me to do what I could to restore the relationship (see Matt. 5:23-24). So I went on from there, and over the next several months the relationship began to change for the better. A year after the incident, I remarked to my wife, "I think our friendship has healed. His deep sense of hurt seems to be gone, and by all appearances, he has forgiven me. In fact, I think our relationship is better than it was before."

Walking in forgiveness is vital to all aspects of personal health and growth. The director of a mental hospital stated at a university seminar that half his patients could go home if they only knew they were forgiven. If you choose not to forgive yourself, be aware that you are not seeing yourself as God sees you. You may feel bad about your sins, but do not allow bad feelings to cloud the truth of God's forgiveness.

Again, your involvement in a body of loving believers will help you see yourself more clearly. Forgiveness is to be a primary trait of relationships among believers. Paul instructed, "Be kind and compassionate to one another, forgiving each other, just as in Christ God forgave you" (Eph. 4:32). The week-by-week experience among believers of forgiving one another and seeking one another's forgiveness will keep God's forgiveness in plain view.

As "royal priests" in the body of Christ (see 1 Peter 2:9), we play a key role in helping each other see ourselves as forgiven, as God sees us. Peter admonished, "Therefore confess your sins to each other and pray for each other so that you may be healed" (James 5:16). We do not believe that a person can absolve another person of sin; God alone forgives sin. Yet as we confess our sins to one another and pray for one another, we do have the priestly responsibility of assuring each other of God's forgiveness. That should be the final word whenever Christians gather to deal with their sin. "You have confessed it, we have prayed about it, God has forgiven it. Go in peace. You are forgiven!" Such ministry is a direct route to 20/20 vision concerning our worthiness to God.

GETTING A CLEARER PICTURE OF YOUR IDENTITY

Part of understanding who you are involves understanding who God is and experiencing his heart toward you. Reflect on the following truths about God. Take time to write your responses to the questions in a notebook or journal.

1. *God is holy.* We read in Psalm 22:3: "You are holy. The praises of Israel surround your throne" (NLT).
   - What does it mean to you that God is holy?
   - What does it mean to you that a holy God finds you valuable?

2. *God is good.* We read in Psalm 119:68: "You are good and do only good; teach me your principles" (NLT).
   - What does it mean to you that God is totally good, unable to do anything wrong?

- What does it mean to you that this good God declares you immensely valuable?

A second part of understanding who you are involves hearing what God says about who *you* are. Listen to God's voice speaking to you:

1. *God says, "You are valuable."* We read in 1 Corinthians 6:19-20: "You do not belong to yourself, for God bought you with a high price" (NLT).
   - Take this verse and personalize it: "I am so valuable to God that he bought me at a high price."
   - What does it mean to you that God loves you enough to have paid a high price for you—not because of anything you have done, but just because he finds you valuable?
   - Do you sense God's heart toward you as he has given the life of his precious Son to show you how valuable you are to him?

2. *God says, "You are a member of Christ's body."* We read in 1 Corinthians 12:27: "Now all of you together are Christ's body, and each one of you is a separate and necessary part of it" (NLT).
   - Take this verse and personalize it: "I am a necessary part of Christ's body—of Christ himself."
   - What does it mean to you that you are necessary to God?
   - Do you sense God's heart toward you as he has drawn you to himself and made you part of his body?

Take time to thank God for what he has revealed about himself to you. Listen to him as he speaks these words to your heart throughout the coming days and weeks. Let these truths from Scripture work their way deep into your heart and your identity.

CHAPTER 12

A New Sense of Competence

R on is the senior pastor of a growing, 1,500-member church. He directs the ministry of a very busy staff, moderates a large ruling board, and preaches three services on Sunday morning.

But Ron is also a devoted father. In the early days of their family, Ron and his wife, Jorie, decided to commit priority time and resources to help each child discover and excel in at least one field of personal interest. They wanted to equip their children for success in life by nurturing a sense of competence and self-confidence.

Since Ron and Jorie are avid tennis players, it was no surprise that three of their four older sons showed an early interest in and ability for the sport. They joined an athletic club so their boys could take advantage of tennis lessons and year-round tournaments. Tad, David, and Joel worked their way up in the national rankings for their respective age groups. Ron and Jorie attended as many matches and tournaments as they possibly could, sometimes traveling across the country to cheer their sons on in a national junior tennis tournament.

But their third son was not as interested in tennis as his brothers. Luke loved horses, so Ron and Jorie became his biggest supporters. On Luke's eleventh birthday, they bought him a horse. Their son was absolutely shocked. Luke saved his allowance and eventually bought another horse. After breeding them, Luke, now sixteen, has five horses. Ron and Jorie were so committed to Luke's growing sense of competence that they sold their house and moved the family to a rural site where he could keep his horses.

All four sons continue to enjoy and excel in their chosen interests as their parents lovingly and sacrificially support them. The boys are growing into young adulthood with a clear sense that they are lovable, valuable, and competent people. Ron and Jorie plan to follow the same course with the four additional children they have adopted into their family.

Did you have parents anything like this couple? As a child, were you encouraged in your interests to the point that you see yourself as skillful and competent in a few areas of life today? Or did you grow up feeling as if you were all thumbs at everything you tried because the significant adults in your life showed little confidence in your abilities? Perhaps these negative influences from your childhood and youth have been magnified in adulthood because many people around you fail to see you as competent. Or perhaps a number of unfortunate failures in your life—a lost job, a failed friendship or marriage, a rebellious child—have left you feeling that *you* are a failure.

The third foundational pillar to true identity is to see ourselves as competent in Christ. That is how God sees us. Paul was not brash or boastful to proclaim, "For I can do everything with the help of Christ who gives me the strength I need" (Phil. 4:13, NLT). He simply saw himself as gifted and equipped to serve God, and that is how we are to see ourselves. This does not mean that you are destined to be a replica of the apostle Paul, and it does not mean that you will excel at every endeavor in life. Rather, God wants you to see that he has given you certain physical, mental, and spiritual abilities and that he has equipped you to use those abilities successfully. What's more, God is so confident in your abilities that he has called you to fulfill his great commission. Your sense of identity will be transformed when you grasp the truth that God sees you as competent and useful.

LIVING THE IMPOSSIBLE LIFE IN THE COMPETENCE OF THE SPIRIT

The key to transforming a poor sense of competence is your relationship with God the Holy Spirit. The Bible has much to say about our relationship with the Holy Spirit.

- We are born again of the Spirit (John 3:3-5).
- The Spirit lives within us and will be with us forever (John 14:16-17).
- The Spirit teaches us what we need to know (John 14:26).
- The Spirit testifies to us that we belong to God (Rom. 8:16).
- The Spirit guides us (Rom. 8:14).
- The Spirit equips us with talents, abilities, and spiritual gifts so that we can live purposeful lives in God's service (1 Cor. 12:4, 11).
- The Spirit helps us in times of weakness, interceding for us (Rom. 8:26-27).
- The Spirit develops in us the fruit of God's righteousness: love, joy, peace, patience, kindness, goodness, faithfulness, gentleness, and self-control (Gal. 5:22-23).

The most direct route to seeing your competence in the Holy Spirit is to understand the resources available to you as a result of the Spirit's indwelling presence in your life. Something wonderful and miraculous happened to Christ's followers on the Day of Pentecost, ten days after he ascended into heaven. They were filled with the Holy Spirit and went forth in his power to change the course of history. The same Holy Spirit who empowered the disciples to live holy lives and become effective witnesses two millennia ago desires to work in us today. The fact that Jesus Christ lives in us by the power of his Spirit and expresses his love through us to the world is one of the most important truths in the Word of God.

Living out the biblical standards for the Christian life by ourselves is impossible, and trying to do so—and failing, as we inevitably do—is bound to cloud our sense of competence as God's children. In fact, Christians who try by their own power to be as much like Christ as possible may have a poorer sense of competence and usefulness than the non-Christian who lives by human ideals. Biblical standards are too lofty for us to achieve on our own. Only one person has been able to succeed at keeping them: Jesus Christ. The Christian life was meant to be lived only in the power of his Holy Spirit. Without him we have every reason to sense that we are incompetent in his service.

Jesus pointed to the Spirit's key role in our competence when he told his disciples, "You will receive power when the Holy Spirit comes on you; and you will be my witnesses in Jerusalem, and in all Judea and Samaria, and to the ends of the earth" (Acts 1:8). Apart from the Holy Spirit, it is impossible not only to become a Christian but also to produce the fruit of the Spirit and to introduce others to Christ. Jesus was referring to the Spirit as well as to himself when he said flatly, "Apart from me you can do nothing" (John 15:5).

From the moment we receive Christ and are indwelled by the Holy Spirit, everything we need to be competent and effective for Christ is available to us. The key lies in allowing the Holy Spirit to fill us daily so we can implement all he has placed at our disposal. Paul conveys this in his command, "Be filled with the Spirit" (Eph. 5:18). Literally translated, the verse reads, "Keep on allowing yourself to be filled with the Spirit." For the Christian, day-by-day competence requires day-by-day filling.

Being filled with the Spirit daily does not mean that you need more of the Holy Spirit coming into you from the outside. Rather, it means allowing the Holy Spirit who is already in you to occupy more of your life. This is why I prefer to use words like being *permeated* or *empowered* by the Spirit. Day-by-day filling with the Spirit means day-by-day empowering to live for Christ and be his witnesses.

We are empowered with the Spirit by faith in an all-powerful God, who loves us. Since he commands us to be filled with the Spirit, he will fill us when we open ourselves to him. You can count on it. It is like withdrawing money from the bank when you have plenty in your account. You don't approach the bank teller with panic, afraid that your withdrawal request will be denied. You don't have to beg the teller to give you the money. Rather, you go to the bank "in faith," place the withdrawal slip on the counter, and receive the money that is already yours. Similarly, receiving the Holy Spirit on a daily basis is simply a matter of appropriating something you already have.

GOD'S PLAN FOR BEING EMPOWERED

While you may withdraw your money at the bank by faith, you must recognize that there are certain procedures for making a withdrawal. For example, you cannot stand on the curb outside the bank and yell, "I want my money!" and expect to be served. You must fill out a withdrawal slip and present it at the teller's window. Similarly, there are some vital steps of preparation for the day-by-day experience of being empowered by the Holy Spirit.

1. You must be hungry and thirsty for God and desire to be filled with his Spirit. Jesus said, "Blessed are those who hunger and thirst for righteousness, for they will be filled" (Matt. 5:6). You are "hungry" for God when you are aware of your helplessness without him. If you are not hungry, you are already full of your own competence instead of the Spirit's. And if you are already full, you have no desire to receive.

2. *Surrender the direction and control of your life to Christ.* Paul wrote, "Dear brothers and sisters, I plead with you to give your bodies to God. Let them be a living and holy sacrifice—the kind he will accept. When you think of what he has done for you, is this too much to ask?" (Rom. 12:1, NLT). In order for God to equip you with his competence, you must relinquish your own attempts to run your life.

3. *Confess every sin the Holy Spirit brings to your mind and accept the cleansing and forgiveness God promises.* The wonderful promise in 1 John 1:9 reminds us: "If we confess our sins to him, he is faithful and just to forgive us and to cleanse us from every wrong" (NLT). Daily empowerment by the Holy Spirit requires daily confession and cleansing.

Being filled with the Spirit is not an option for the believer; it is a command. God commands us to be filled with his Spirit (Eph. 5:18). Yet God never issues a command without also providing a way for us to obey him. He makes the promise, "This is the confidence we have in approaching God: that if we ask anything according to his will, he hears us. And if we know that he hears us—whatever we ask—we know that we have what we asked of him" (1 John 5:14-15). All we must do is ask God to fill us, and since we know he hears us, we can be confident he will fill us.

When you ask to be filled with the Holy Spirit, you are not asking the Spirit to come into your life. He is already there. Christians are *indwelled* by the Holy Spirit only once, at the time Christ comes into our lives through his Spirit. But we are to be *filled* repeatedly. We ask the indwelling Holy Spirit to fill and control every part of our lives, every hidden corner and crevice. As we do, we tap into his competence. The frustration and futility of self-effort is eliminated when we live in the power of the Holy Spirit.

He imparts to us the ability to live a holy life and to serve God effectively with the abilities he has given.

Do you desire a life filled with the Spirit and his competence? You need only ask the Father for it. Acknowledge that you have been in control of your life, which is sin against God, the rightful ruler of your life. Thank him for forgiving your sins through Christ's death on the cross for you. Invite Christ to take control of your life, and invite his Spirit to empower you so you can glorify Christ in all you do. Then thank him for doing what you have asked. You are not being presumptuous to thank God before you actually experience the result of your request. It is an act of faith that he keeps his promise to give us whatever we ask within his will. And since he commands us to be filled with the Holy Spirit, we know it is his will that we ask and receive. So it is entirely appropriate to thank him for what he will do.

The apostle Paul, exulting in the sense of competence he enjoyed through the Holy Spirit's empowering, said, "I can do everything with the help of Christ who gives me the strength I need" (Phil. 4:13, NLT). The emphasis was not on what Paul could do but on what Christ—the source of his strength—can do. Paul attempted great things *for* God because he expected great things *from* God. And so can we because, "not that we are competent in ourselves to claim anything for ourselves, but our competence comes from God" (2 Cor. 3:5).

GOD CAN TURN OUR INCOMPETENCE INTO COMPETENCE

Carl was a very skilled and successful investment accounts manager for a major financial institution. As board members of the church Carl attended got better acquainted with him, they remarked to each other, "This man would be a great addition to our church budget committee. He has extensive education and experience in finance. He knows how to manage money successfully.

He would be a natural." Soon afterward Carl was invited to serve on the committee. He accepted, eager to contribute something to his church.

Carl's first few months on the committee were a disaster. The apparent strength he brought to the task turned out to be a glaring weakness. Relying on his financial training, he evaluated all church expenditures by the "bottom line." If a certain church program did not show a "profit" of numerical or financial growth, he argued that it should be cut. He regarded ministries that did not show a strong visible return—such as missions projects that did not directly benefit the church—as a waste. It soon became clear to church leaders that Carl lacked the spiritual gift of faith necessary for investing church tithes and offerings. After a discussion with his wise and loving pastor, Carl resigned his committee position.

Carl could have looked at this experience and concluded that he was worthless, that he was not able to take his area of expertise and use it for God. But Carl's pastor encouraged him to think that even though his financial skills did not work on the budget committee, God would show him how he could serve.

Carl did not give up. As he continued to grow in his faith and yield control of his life to the Holy Spirit, he sensed that he might like to work as a volunteer in the junior high ministry. He had never worked with kids before and had no training in youth ministry. But his heart was burdened for the youth-group kids who came from non-Christian homes. He was surprised to learn that his wife, Brenda, felt the same burden.

After much prayer, Carl and Brenda met with the youth pastor. "We don't know a thing about youth work," they said, "but we love these kids and we're willing to learn. If you can use us, we are available." The youth pastor invited them to join the ministry team as volunteers.

The couple took to youth ministry as a bird takes to flight. They opened their home to junior high students for Bible studies and just "hanging out." The kids flocked to Carl and Brenda because they felt genuinely loved and accepted. Carl and Brenda laughed and had fun with the kids, and they cried with those who were hurting. The junior high group continues to grow because of Carl and Brenda's willingness to let the Spirit of God call them to and empower them in a ministry for which they are "unskilled."

When you look at the people God uses, you often find that even though they have limitations, when they submit their lives to the Holy Spirit, God equips them for ministry. It may not always be in their apparent area of expertise, as was the case with Carl.

God is not limited by your limitations.

Seeing yourself as God sees you does not mean you are without limitations or weaknesses. Even Spirit-controlled people are imperfect and candidates for growth. Rather, seeing yourself as God sees you means seeing yourself as competent despite your limitations or weaknesses. God is not limited by your limitations. His cause is not weakened by your weaknesses. What's more, God is not impressed with your abilities, as if his work is crippled without you. Whoever you are and wherever you are in your Christian growth, God will use you if you allow his Spirit to empower you daily. As you walk the Spirit-filled life, you can be confident that "God, who began the good work within you, will continue his work until it is finally finished on that day when Christ Jesus comes back again" (Phil. 1:6, NLT).

GETTING A CLEARER PICTURE OF YOUR IDENTITY
Part of understanding who you are involves understanding who God is and experiencing his heart toward you. Reflect on the

following truths about God. Take time to write your responses to the questions in a notebook or journal.

1. *God is everywhere.* We read in Psalm 139:7-10: "I can never escape from your spirit! I can never get away from your presence! If I go up to heaven, you are there; if I go down to the place of the dead, you are there. If I ride the wings of the morning, if I dwell by the farthest oceans, even there your hand will guide me, and your strength will support me" (NLT).
    * What does it mean to you that everywhere you go, God is there to guide you and strengthen you?
    * Can you feel God's love for you in his commitment to be everywhere with you?

2. *God is all-powerful.* We read in Job 42:2: "I know that you can do anything, and no one can stop you" (NLT).
    * What does it mean to you that God can do anything?
    * What does it mean to you that an all-powerful God has given you everything you need to be a competent member of his family?

A second part of understanding who you are involves hearing what God says about who *you* are. Listen to God's voice speaking to you:

1. *God says, "You are selected to be fruitful."* We read in John 15:16: "You didn't choose me. I chose you. I appointed you to go and produce fruit that will last" (NLT).
    * Take this verse and personalize it: "God has chosen me to be fruitful."
    * What does it mean to you that God has chosen you and has equipped you to be a competent person?

- Do you sense God's heart toward you in trusting you with his work?

2. *God says, "You are equipped."* We read in 1 Corinthians 1:7: "Now you have every spiritual gift you need as you eagerly wait for the return of our Lord Jesus Christ" (NLT).
   - Take this verse and personalize it: "God has provided me with everything I need to serve him."
   - What does it mean to you that God values you enough to equip you for serving him?
   - Do you sense God's heart toward you in giving you everything you need to be competent?

Take time to thank God for what he has revealed about himself to you. Listen to him as he speaks these words to your heart throughout the coming days and weeks. Let these truths from Scripture work their way deep into your heart and your identity.

PART
FIVE
Gaining a New Identity

CHAPTER 13

Seeking a Transformational Environment

Many Christians I talk to have taken hold of God's fullness the best they know how, and yet years later they have a woefully inadequate view of who they really are in Christ. Maybe you are one of those Christians. God may have used you in wonderful ways in the past. Perhaps you are revered by many as the epitome of faith and spiritual maturity. But you still see yourself as a poor specimen of God's creation. You have difficulty believing that God or anyone else would consider you lovable, valuable, or competent.

We have already discussed from Scripture how God sees you and why you have every right to see yourself as lovable, valuable, and competent. But how does it happen? What kind of environment encourages people to see themselves differently?

You acquire a new sense of identity the same way you acquired your current sense of identity. You grew up seeing yourself as unlovable, unworthy, or incompetent because your environment—particularly the significant people around you—conveyed that message to you. In order to transform your sense of identity, you must put yourself in an environment where the truth about who you are abounds. You must allow yourself to be positively influenced by people who see themselves and you through God's eyes. As you are exposed to an atmosphere permeated with the truth about who you are, your faulty inner portrait will be transformed.

In chapter 9 we looked at the story of Jesus raising Lazarus from the dead. When Lazarus emerged from the tomb, he was still shrouded in graveclothes. Jesus, choosing to use other people to fulfill his purposes for Lazarus, instructed Lazarus's friends and family to unwrap him from the graveclothes that bound him. In much the same way, God chooses to use other believers to help you get free from the bondage of your inaccurate sense of your identity. He uses other Christians to be the agents of transformation.

In order to transform your sense of identity, you must put yourself in an environment where the truth about who you are abounds.

AN ENVIRONMENT SATURATED WITH THE TRUTH

What does this ideal, transformational environment look like?

1. A transformational environment will include people who model the truth about who you are in Christ. You need to spend quality and quantity time with people who see clearly that they are loved, valued, and useful to God and others. These people will not necessarily be the busiest people for God. Christian "workaholics" are often overly busy because they are trying to earn God's approval instead of confidently walking in it. Good role models of a true sense of identity radiate an intimate relationship with God and genuinely enjoy serving him. These models may or may not be gifted with social skills, but they are comfortable around people because they are confident about their identity. Many of these people are involved in discipling or mentoring other believers either formally or informally.

2. A transformational environment is one in which the truth about your identity is clearly taught from the Scriptures. Perhaps when you were a child it was drummed into you by a parent, teacher, or other significant adult that you were worthless. That information about who you are is inaccurate. You need to be taught the scriptural truth about how God sees you. You need to be around Bible teachers, Bible study leaders, and other mature Christians who declare through their lessons and conversations your scriptural acceptance and worth in God's eyes.

3. *A transformational environment provides a context of loving, intimate relationships.* As believers *model* the truth, you will *observe* people regarding one another as lovable, valuable, and competent. As believers *teach* the truth, you will *learn* from Scripture that God sees you as lovable, valuable, and competent. But as you *relate* to people who understand their true identity, you will *experience* the truth personally. It is in the context of caring Christian relationships that people express love to one another, value one another, and serve one another in practical ways.

As an example, consider this scenario: Just before you leave work for the day, your boss calls you in and announces that you are being passed over for the promotion and raise you were expecting. A newer employee with advanced training has been given priority. Driving home, you are really bummed out. Old feelings of inadequacy and failure tempt you to skip your Bible study group that meets this evening. But somehow you know you should go even though you would rather crawl into a hole and wallow in self-pity.

When you tell your good friends at Bible study about your misfortune, they surround you with comfort and care. You know their love is genuine because they have supported you and encouraged you in the past. And you have done the same for many of them during difficult times. They remind you that you are still skilled and useful, not only to the company for which you work, but also to the group.

During Bible study, one group member points out in the passage under discussion the reminders that God sees us as useful members of his body. He reminds the group that you spent a weekend recently helping his family move into a new apartment. He affirms your spiritual gift of service. You leave the group knowing that you are loved, appreciated, and needed in the group. The nurturing relationships here help you see clearly that you are a person of worth and usefulness to God and others. You always go away with a better picture of who you are.

It is vital that you are involved in an ongoing, loving, mutually supportive relationship with other believers.

This is the kind of environment that can transform the distorted inner portrait you have carried from childhood. It is vital that you are involved in an ongoing, loving, mutually supportive relationship with other believers. It may be an adult Sunday school class, a neighborhood Bible study group, or a home group from your church. The group must be small enough that you can get to know a number of people on an intimate level. Merely sitting in a church pew for an hour on Sunday morning does not allow for much relationship building. Plant yourself in a small group where consistent, loving interaction reinforces the truth of who God says you are.

GOD'S PROGRAM FOR TRANSFORMATION

The program God designed to help us transform our sense of identity is seen in the description of the early church:

> They joined with the other believers and devoted themselves to the apostles' teaching and fellowship, sharing in

the Lord's Supper and in prayer. A deep sense of awe came over them all, and the apostles performed many miraculous signs and wonders. And all the believers met together constantly and shared everything they had. They sold their possessions and shared the proceeds with those in need. They worshiped together at the Temple each day, met in homes for the Lord's Supper, and shared their meals with great joy and generosity—all the while praising God and enjoying the goodwill of all the people. And each day the Lord added to their group those who were being saved (Acts 2:42-47, NLT).

The emphasis here and throughout the New Testament seems to be on three experiences in which every believer is to take part. Notice how these three elements correspond to the threefold environment of transformation just described.

1. *Every believer needs to be involved in a vital teaching experience.* The first-century church was devoted to the teaching of God's Word, and we must be also. We study the Bible not primarily to learn what to *do* as Christians but how to *be* as Christians. As we understand from Scripture who we are and what we are becoming, the doing part of our faith will practically take care of itself.

2. *Every believer needs to be involved in a vital relational experience.* The Jerusalem believers were as much devoted to the fellowship—being together, praying together, eating together—as they were to the study of the Word. This is where they experienced the Word day by day. This is where they learned to treat each other as lovable, valuable, competent members of God's family.

3. *Every believer needs to be involved in a vital witnessing relationship.* We observe through the positive example of other believers what it means to be loved and valued by God. But people who are not Christians also need to know that God loves and values them. According to the New Testament, witnessing consists of living

the truth of who we are in Christ and then talking about it whenever possible. That is how people were added to the church on a daily basis in the early church. Modeling our identity as loved, valued, competent children of God is a primary vehicle for proclaiming the gospel of salvation.

First Thessalonians 2:1-12 provides an excellent example of how the apostle Paul put this process into operation among believers. He described how he treated the believers in Thessalonica with the tenderness of a nursing mother (see v. 7). He described how he exhorted them and encouraged them as a father (see. v. 11). He emphasized his relationship with them: "We loved you so much that we were delighted to share with you not only the gospel of God but our lives as well, because you had become so dear to us" (v. 8).

Paul's involvement in the transformation process is evident in this passage. He *taught* the new converts the truth about how God sees them. He *related* to them in love and understanding. And he *witnessed* to them or *modeled* for them what it means to be a godly person with a proper sense of identity.

Twice in this passage Paul calls his readers *brothers* even though, as an apostle, he could have taken an authoritative posture. This is an important distinction to keep in mind regarding our relationships in the body of Christ. Each of us is both a learner and a teacher. Sometimes you may think you are always on the giving end or always on the receiving end. But a relationship of brothers and sisters in Christ always works two ways. In a transformational environment, everyone gives and receives, ministers and receives ministry.

"This process sounds like discipleship," you may say. Yes, the transformation of our sense of identity is wrapped up in the discipleship process. Yet we often view discipleship as learning how to live the Christian life. In its broadest sense, discipleship is the process of learning how to *be* a Christian. You need to know who you are before you can understand how to live. I hope that you are involved with a body of believers whose goal in modeling, teaching, and relating the truth is becoming who we are as much as doing what we should.

GOD'S WORD IN THE PROCESS OF TRANSFORMATION

The Holy Spirit works through a body of believers and his holy Word to help us see ourselves as God sees us. Peter wrote, "Like newborn babies, crave pure spiritual milk, so that by it you may grow up in your salvation, now that you have tasted that the Lord is good" (1 Pet. 2:2-3). God's Word is his primary agent in renewing our minds to think as he thinks and see as he sees (see Rom. 12:2).

Notice how the ministry of the Word through others is designed to produce in us maturity, which begins with a mature concept of who we are:

> It was he who gave some to be apostles, some to be prophets, some to be evangelists, and some to be pastors and teachers, to prepare God's people for works of service, so that the body of Christ may be built up until we all reach unity in the faith and in the knowledge of the Son of God and become mature, attaining to the whole measure of the fullness of Christ.
>
> Then we will no longer be infants, tossed back and forth by the waves, and blown here and there by every wind of teaching and by the cunning and craftiness of men in their deceitful scheming. Instead, speaking the truth in love, we will in all things grow up into him who is the Head, that is, Christ (Eph. 4:11-15).

Through his Word, God reveals his attributes, character, and personality. Through Christ's body, the church, God makes these qualities real and tangible to us. Jesus told his disciples, "Anyone

171

who has seen me has seen the Father. . . . Don't you believe that I am in the Father, and that the Father is in me? The words I say to you are not just my own. Rather, it is the Father, living in me, who is doing his work" (John 14:9-10). In his human form, Jesus revealed God in a way we could understand. For example, God's love is clearly seen in Christ's compassion for his disciples, for the hurting, and for the lost.

Jesus made the character and attributes of God real. He put flesh and bones to God's personality. We know what God is like because Jesus made him known to us. We know that we are loved, valued, and useful to God because that is how Jesus related to people. Could it be that the purpose of the church is to reveal God's character as Jesus did? The answer is *yes!* We as Christ's body are to demonstrate the character and attributes of God the Father to one another and to the world. How better to know that we are loved and valued by God than to be loved and valued in the flesh by his people? How better to see ourselves as God sees us than to have loving believers tell us and show us what God sees? It is one thing to read about God in the Scriptures or hear about him in a sermon. It is even more real when we experience God through the members of his church.

APPLYING GOD'S PROGRAM TO YOUR NEED

Our inner portraits are transformed as we submit ourselves to God's program for realizing our true identity. Here are a few simple steps to help you apply God's program to your individual situation.

1. Pinpoint your specific need. Which of the three pillars of your identity seems most in need of transformation? More specifically, which of the following do you find most difficult to accept: God loves you just as you are and wants you for his child (you are lovable); God would have sent Jesus to die for you even if you were the only person on earth (you are valuable); God trusts you to reach out and minister to others (you are useful)? Does one area seem to stand out when you ponder these questions? It may be the first area to work on.

If you have difficulty coming up with one area to work on, pray about it. Ask God to impress on your heart the specific area of your inner portrait he desires to bring into conformity with how he sees you. Pray with confidence and hope. Remember, he is the One who knows you best and loves you most! He desires that your perception of your identity become more like his perception of you. You may want to begin your prayer by using the petition of the psalmist: "Search me, O God, and know my heart; test me and know my thoughts. Point out anything in me that offends you, and lead me along the path of everlasting life" (Ps. 139:23-24, NLT).

You may want someone to join you in this search, especially if it uncovers some painful memories or experiences from the past. Consider asking your spouse, a trusted Christian friend, a pastor, or a Christian counselor to pray with you and seek God's transforming work.

2. *Find help from the Scriptures.* Once you have an idea which area is most in need of transformation, begin to study the Scriptures with this need in mind. Whenever you sit down to read, ask God to apply his Word to your heart and mind so you may see yourself as he does. As you study, you will discover verses and phrases that seem tailor-made for your situation. You may read passages you have read numerous times and see something you never noticed before, something just right for you. Specific, goal-oriented Bible study like this helps you see how your inner portrait can change.

The Word of God has the power to transform lives. When you study and meditate on passages of Scripture that apply to specific needs, dramatic results are possible. Often these results can be explained only as supernatural works of the Holy Spirit. The Spirit uses the Word of God to restructure and transform how we see ourselves.

d help from other believers. Finally, allow members of body to be instruments of the Holy Spirit in your trans- tion. We are instructed in Galatians 6:2, "Carry each *'s* burdens, and in this way you will fulfill the law of Christ." You are not the only Christian who needs a clearer picture of your true identity. We are all in the process of learning to see our- selves as God sees us. Paul admonishes us to assist one another in this pursuit. How? Any way we can. But it can happen only if we confide in one another about our burdens. That means you must be willing to share your difficult burdens with others and seek their help as well as lend your support to those around you who are hurting. You must be transparent, telling others about your struggles. You must let others love and care for you just as you love and care for them.

Through the caring interaction of the body of Christ, we expe- rience God's love and attributes personally. As we relate to one another according to his program, we become the beneficiaries of his character and personality to the point that our lives are trans- formed. Our relationships with other believers are a catalyst for healing in our lives. For example, as I receive God's comfort, mercy, and forgiveness through you, I begin to see myself as God sees me. As you receive God's acceptance and encouragement through me, you see yourself more clearly as God sees you. Treated as a person of value and worth, I will see myself as valued and wor- thy. Treated as a trustworthy person, you will develop greater con- fidence in yourself as God's child. Our inner portraits are transformed as the Holy Spirit uses each of us to reveal Christ to the other.

The ongoing process of mutual love and acceptance produces an upward spiral of transformation in the body of Christ. The more we see ourselves as God sees us, the easier it is to accept that we are loved, valued, and useful. The greater our acceptance of who we are, the easier it is to respond to others with love and acceptance. As others sense God's love and acceptance through us, they become more confident that they are loved, valued, and useful to God. They in turn grow as ministers of God's love and acceptance to us. And so the process of ministry continues as we "spur one another on toward love and good deeds" (Heb. 10:24).

It is in the context of this transformational environment that we are exposed to increasing amounts of God's light. As the light of God's truth floods into our lives, we cannot help but see ourselves as God sees us, which is exactly what he has in mind.

GETTING A CLEARER PICTURE OF YOUR IDENTITY
Part of understanding who you are involves understanding who God is and experiencing his heart toward you. Reflect on the following truths about God. Take time to write your responses to the questions in a notebook or journal.

> 1. *God is patient.* We read in Romans 2:4: "Don't you realize how kind, tolerant, and patient God is with you?" (NLT).
>   - What does it mean to you that God is patient?
>   - What does it mean to you that a patient God wants you to grow and experience his love for you through the love and care of other believers?
>
> 2. *God is caring.* We read in Psalm 103:4: "He ransoms me from death and surrounds me with love and tender mercies" (NLT).
>   - What does it mean to you that God surrounds you with love and tender mercies?
>   - What does it mean to you that God cares so much about your wholeness that he surrounds you with loving and tender people?

A second part of understanding who you are involves hearing what God says about who *you* are. Listen to God's voice speaking to you:

1. God says, *"You are special."* We read in Deuteronomy 4:20: "Remember that the Lord rescued you . . . to become his own people and special possession; that is what you are today" (NLT).
   - Take this verse and personalize it: "God rescued me so that I would be his own, his special possession. I can say with confidence that I am God's special possession."
   - What does it mean to you that God wanted you for his own special child?
   - Do you sense God's heart toward you in rescuing you and making you special?

2. God says, *"You are growing."* We read in 1 Thessalonians 3:12: "May the Lord make your love grow and overflow to each other and to everyone else, just as our love overflows toward you" (NLT).
   - Take this verse and personalize it: "The Lord will cause my love to grow and overflow to the people around me, just as the love of other believers overflows toward me."
   - What does it mean to you that God wants you to grow and will cause it to happen in you?
   - Do you sense God's heart toward you in helping you grow to be more like himself?

Take time to thank God for what he has revealed about himself to you. Listen to him as he speaks these words to your heart throughout the coming days and weeks. Let these truths from Scripture work their way deep into your heart and your identity.

176

CHAPTER 14

The Broader View
of Who You Are

When we looked in chapter 9 at the story of how Jesus brought Lazarus back to life, we noted that Jesus made Lazarus alive and then commanded his friends and his family to unwrap him so that he would be free. But free for what? What was the purpose of Lazarus's freedom?

Let's ask that same question about ourselves. What is the purpose of our restored perception of our identity? Is it just to make us feel better about ourselves? Is it just to make us feel whole? Is it just to make us free for freedom's sake?

No. God has a much deeper purpose for restoring our faulty self-portrait. He wants us to be utterly convinced that we are loved, valuable, and competent because he has work for us to do.

Do you realize that you and I are God's gift to the world? If not, we have no reason to be here. It would have made more sense for God to take us straight to heaven the moment we trusted Christ. The fact that he leaves us on earth even after we belong to him tells us that we are gifts to humanity, that we have a distinct purpose for being here. Our purpose is connected to how God sees us and how we are to see ourselves. It is vital to our sense of identity that we understand our purpose in life.

Bob is an executive "headhunter," a person who aggressively seeks out and hires corporation executives for other firms. He was explaining to me one day how he interviews prospects. "Josh, when I find executives that I want to get to know, I like to disarm them. I bring them into my office and offer them a drink. Then I take off my coat, loosen my tie, and put my feet up on the desk. I ask them about their interests: sports, hiking, books, family, or whatever it is. When they look relaxed and totally nonthreatened, I lean over, look them squarely in the eye, and ask, 'What is your purpose in life?' It's amazing how top executives fall apart when they hear that question. They don't know how to answer."

Bob went on. "But one prospect I interviewed the other day really surprised me. I had my feet up on the desk, and I was talking with him about football. He was all relaxed. Then I zoomed in with my killer question: 'What is your purpose in life, Nathan?' Nathan returned my look and, without blinking an eye, said, 'My purpose in life is to go to heaven and take as many people with me as I can.' For the first time in my career, I was speechless!"

I love Nathan's response, and I have used it myself many times. Nathan realized that he had been "unwrapped" so that he could "unwrap" others. Nathan knew that Christ had made him alive and set him free so that he would be equipped to be part of Christ's body as it set others free too.

A good sense of your true identity as God's loved, valued, and competent child should generate a desire to become part of God's redemptive plan. When you grasp the concept that God created everyone in his image and sent Christ to die for everyone, you want to share his love with them. Like Nathan, you are not satisfied to be on your way to heaven. You want to take with you others for whom Christ died. It is our purpose for being here.

You may say, "But Josh, very few, if any, people have come to Christ directly from my telling them about him." That may be true. But it is likely that a number of people are on their way to trusting Christ because of who you are in Christ and how you relate to them in his love. You do not have to lead unbelievers to the altar to fulfill your purpose. The way you live will point to something different about who you are. If as a Christian you see yourself as God's loved, valued, and competent child, you are communicating something of the gospel to others. As you add to your *living witness* the element of a *telling witness*—speaking about Christ when the opportunities arise—you will likely see even more people come to Christ through your efforts.

God wants us to be utterly convinced that we are loved, valuable, and competent because he has work for us to do.

WITNESSING: THE OVERFLOW OF WHO WE ARE

Our Christian training has drummed into many of us that we ought to share Christ with others. For those of us who do not have a clear sense of who we are as God's loved, valued, and competent children, the challenge to witness only produces greater guilt as the years pass by and we have not seen anyone come to Christ through us. In fact, the inner portrait seems even more distorted because we suspect that God loves us less for our lack of fruitfulness as his witnesses.

Many Christians are convinced that their lives are not good enough for them be a verbal witness. "I have to get my act together first before I can tell others about Christ," they say. The problem is that we will never get our act completely together. So these people go through life trying to live lives that are "good enough," and they always fall short, leading to guilt, frustration, and hopelessness. Other people are afraid of the negative reactions they may receive when they tell others about Christ. They don't want to offend people or make them angry, so they say nothing. Others are convinced they will bungle their attempts to share the gospel, leaving the hearers more confused.

Fears and excuses like these are a dead giveaway that witnessing is seen primarily as something we *do* instead of that which flows from who we *are*. And a focus on doing reflects a poor sense of identity in Christ because Christianity is more about *being* than about *doing*. If one of the fears mentioned above characterizes your response to witnessing, it may reveal an area where your sense of identity needs to be transformed.

If you feel that you are not "good enough" to witness for Christ, you have a limited sense of God's love for you. The more you see yourself as God sees you—unconditionally accepted, forgiven, created in his image—the less you will see your imperfections as a hindrance. Be aware that God loves you and wants to use you even while you are "in process" as a maturing Christian. If God waited for us to reach total maturity before sending us out to share the gospel with people, he would have to wait until we get to heaven! Furthermore, if we were all perfect, those to whom we share Christ would be discouraged, thinking they could never measure up to our standard. Rather, God's love and witness flows more freely from those who see themselves as loved and accepted in spite of their imperfections.

If you are afraid of the negative reactions you may receive when witnessing, you have a limited sense of your worth to God. Being overly dependent on others for approval suggests that you have a low view of your intrinsic value to the Creator. What are you afraid of? God thinks so highly of you that he allowed his Son to die for you. You are loved and valued by the King of the universe. Even if everyone you know refuses to listen to you, you are still of high value to God. Fear of how others will react to your witness should drive you prayerfully to build up that second pillar of your identity, your worth to God.

If you are reluctant to witness because you fear you will say the wrong thing or stumble over your words, you have a limited sense of your usefulness to God and your competence in him. In a sense, you are saying to God, "I know you want me to witness, but you will have to use somebody more skilled and confident because I am neither." The emphasis in witnessing is not on what you say or how well you say it. Rather, it is on who you are as God's beloved child. You are unique and useful to him just as you are. No one else among the more than six billion people in the world is like you. God knows your skills and your weaknesses, and he can use you no matter how incompetent you feel at times. All you need to pray is, "God, I want to be just what you created me to be. I will share my faith the best I know how and leave the outcome to you."

EARNING THE RIGHT TO BE HEARD

A significant element of sharing Christ with the world is simply doing good to others. Throughout the Scriptures we are admonished to do for others what is right and good. Paul instructed, "If we do what helps [others], we will build them up in the Lord" (Rom. 15:2, NLT). Elsewhere he wrote, "Therefore, as we have opportunity, let us do good to all people, especially to those who belong to the family of believers" (Gal. 6:10). He encouraged us, "Never tire of doing what is right" (2 Thess. 3:13), and "Let us not become weary in doing good" (Gal. 6:9). When we do good things for other people, they have an opportunity to see the Savior in us.

In addition to revealing himself through our doing good things for others, God can also show himself to other people when we do our best in every situation. Paul challenged the Galatians, "Be sure to do what you should, for then you will enjoy the personal satisfaction of having done your work well, and you won't need to compare yourself to anyone else" (Gal. 6:4, NLT). Desiring to do your best is not the same as wanting to be the best at something. Trying to be the best means you are comparing yourself to others, which the Bible discourages. Doing your best for others takes the emphasis off you and allows God to be glorified through your actions. When you use your gifts, talents, and abilities in the power of the Holy Spirit, it doesn't matter what other people do. God will use your efforts to draw people to himself.

AT PEACE WITH WHO YOU ARE

One day I boarded a plane and saw something strange. The female flight attendant who was greeting the boarding passengers was holding a dozen beautiful roses. I have been on literally thousands of commercial flights, but I have never before seen a flight attendant holding a bouquet of flowers.

I stopped and said to her, "Did your boyfriend bring you those flowers?"

"No," she said.

"Your husband, then?"

She shook her head.

"Well, then," I pressed, "who did?"

"I bought them for myself," she said, smiling broadly.

I went back to my seat and stowed my carry-on bags, then I went back up front and introduced myself to the flight attendant. During our conversation, I indicated that I was in Christian ministry, and she told me that she was also a believer.

Still curious about the flowers, I said, "Why did you buy yourself a dozen roses?"

She answered immediately. "Because I like myself."

What a tremendous platform for sharing Christ with others! How we perceive ourselves can make all the difference in the effectiveness of our living and spoken witness. As we grow in the peace of knowing that God loves us, values us, and uses us, we become what Paul called "the fragrance of life" to those who are desperately searching for the peace we enjoy as God's children (2 Cor. 2:16).

No one was more at peace with his identity as God's creation than King David. Here is a psalm of praise he wrote in celebration of God's presence, knowledge, and authority over all aspects of his life.

O Lord, you have searched me and you know me.
You know when I sit and when I rise; you perceive my thoughts
* from afar.*
You discern my going out and my lying down; you are familiar
* with all my ways.*
Before a word is on my tongue you know it completely, O Lord.
You hem me in—behind and before; you have laid your hand
* upon me.*
Such knowledge is too wonderful for me, too lofty for me to at-
* tain.*
Where can I go from your Spirit? Where can I flee from your
* presence?*
If I go up to the heavens, you are there; if I make my bed in the
* depths, you are there.*
If I rise on the wings of the dawn, if I settle on the far side of the
* sea,*
even there your hand will guide me, your right hand will hold
* me fast. . . .*
For you created my inmost being; you knit me together in my
* mother's womb.*
I praise you because I am fearfully and wonderfully made; your
* works are wonderful, I know that full well.*
My frame was not hidden from you when I was made in the secret
* place. When I was woven together in the depths of the earth,*
your eyes saw my unformed body.
All the days ordained for me were written in your book before
* one of them came to be.*
How precious to me are your thoughts, O God! How vast is the
* sum of them! (Ps. 139:1-10, 13-17)*

Here are the thoughts of a man who was at peace with himself as God's loved and cherished creation. No wonder God could use him so effectively as Israel's king despite his obvious failures. No wonder his psalms have been such a powerful witness of God's love and salvation over the centuries. David's example suggests to me that a growing knowledge of God and an increasing awareness of how he sees us are indispensable prerequisites to effective witnessing. Memorizing Bible verses and having a step-by-step witnessing plan are important. But these tools are no substitute for the witness that flows from the life of Christians who know who they are in Christ and like themselves because of it.

A ROOM FULL OF FLOWERS

For several years I spent New Year's Eve alone in a motel room in Laguna Beach, California, away from my home and family. In those days I scheduled a busy speaking tour between Christmas and New Year's. I started out on the East Coast, where my family and I spent Christmas with Dottie's parents. The next day I started my week of traveling, speaking at student conferences night and day until I ended up on the West Coast on New Year's Eve. My family was still in New England, and I was emotionally, physically, and spiritually wiped out. Those were among the loneliest nights I have ever experienced.

One year I flew into Southern California and was picked up at the airport by my friend Don Stewart. As we drove through Laguna Canyon on the way to the motel, we passed a roadside stand where a couple was selling flowers from the bed of their truck. I asked Don to stop, and when he did, I got out and bought a huge bouquet of five dozen flowers. It was quite a challenge to squeeze myself and five dozen flowers into Don's little Honda Civic, but somehow I made it.

Don drove on in silence, but I could tell he was wondering

about my strange purchase. I was sure he was thinking, *What is he doing? He's all alone. His wife and children are three thousand miles away. And he is going to a motel room on New Year's Eve—with five dozen flowers! I've known Josh for years. Is he really the Christian leader I think he is?*

We rode in silence for several blocks. Then Don blurted out, "I give up, Josh. Why all the flowers?"

I enthusiastically related the story of the flight attendant who bought herself a dozen roses. I concluded, "These flowers are reminders to me of who God is, what Jesus has done for me, and who I am by God's grace. Tonight I'm going to put these flowers all over my motel room to remind me that God loves me, cares for me, and forgives me, and that I can accept myself as his unique creation. These flowers will help me remain thankful that God has used me this week to share his love with the world, even though I am spending New Year's Eve in a motel room alone."

Maybe the time has come for you to go out and buy yourself a dozen roses. Or perhaps you need to simply say to God, "Thank you for who I am. Thank you for loving me unconditionally, counting me worthy of your Son's sacrifice, and using me to share your love with others. I want to see myself exactly as you see me. I want to see others exactly as you see them. I yield to you my limitations and doubts so you can make me a better instrument to share your love with the world."

GETTING A CLEARER PICTURE OF YOUR IDENTITY

Part of understanding who you are involves understanding who God is and experiencing his heart toward you. Reflect on the following truths about God. Take time to write your responses to the questions in a notebook or journal.

1. *God is extravagant in his love.* We read in Deuteronomy
   7:7-8: "The Lord did not choose you and lavish his love
   on you because you were larger or greater than other na-
   tions. . . . It was simply because the Lord loves you"
   (NLT).
   - What does it mean to you that God lavishes his love
     on you?
   - What does it mean to you that this extravagant God
     wants you to share the overflow of that love with others?

2. *God is sufficient.* We read in Hebrews 13:20-21: "May
   the God of peace, who brought again from the dead our
   Lord Jesus, equip you with all you need for doing his
   will. May he produce in you, through the power of Jesus
   Christ, all that is pleasing to him. . . . To him be glory
   forever and ever. Amen" (NLT).
   - What does it mean to you that God will equip you
     and give you everything you need for doing his will?
   - What does it mean to you that God will produce in
     you all that is pleasing to him?

A second part of understanding who you are involves hearing
what God says about who *you* are. Listen to God's voice speaking
to you:

1. *God says, "You are my witness."* We read in Acts 1:8:
   "You will receive power when the Holy Spirit comes on
   you; and you will be my witnesses."
   - Take this verse and personalize it: "God has sent his
     Holy Spirit into my life. By the power of that Holy
     Spirit, I am a witness to others of all that God has
     done for me."
   - What does it mean to you that your life is a living
     witness of God's love?

186

- Do you sense God's heart toward you in choosing you to be one of his witnesses?

2. *God says, "You are called by God."* We read in Romans 1:6: "You are among those who have been called to belong to Jesus Christ" (NLT).
    - Take this verse and personalize it: "I am called—by the God of the universe—to be his child, to belong to him, and to share his love with others."
    - What does it mean to you that God has called and equipped you to be his witness?
    - Do you sense God's heart toward you in calling you?

Take time to thank God for what he has revealed about himself to you. Listen to him as he speaks these words to your heart throughout the coming days and weeks. Let these truths from Scripture work their way deep into your heart and your identity.

More about Intimate Life Ministries

Several times in this book I have mentioned the work of Dr. David Ferguson. David's ministry has had such a profound effect on me in the past several years that I want you to have every opportunity to be exposed to his work and ministry. David and his wife, Teresa, direct a ministry called Intimate Life Ministries.

WHO AND WHAT IS INTIMATE LIFE MINISTRIES?

Intimate Life Ministries (ILM) is a training and resource ministry whose purpose is to *assist in the development of Great Commandment ministries worldwide.* Great Commandment ministries—ministries that help us love God and our neighbors—are ongoing ministries that deepen our intimacy with God and with others in marriage, family, and the church.

Intimate Life Ministries comprises:

- A network of **churches** seeking to fortify homes and communities with God's love;
- A network of **pastors and other ministry leaders** walking intimately with God and their families and seeking to live vulnerably before their people;
- A team of **accredited trainers** committed to helping churches establish ongoing Great Commandment ministries;

- A team of **professional associates** from ministry and other professional Christian backgrounds, assisting with research, training, and resource development;
- **Christian broadcasters, publishers, media, and other affiliates,** cooperating to see marriages and families reclaimed as divine relationships;
- **Headquarters staff** providing strategic planning, coordination, and support.

HOW CAN INTIMATE LIFE MINISTRIES SERVE YOU?

ILM's Intimate Life Network of Churches is an effective ongoing support and equipping relationship with churches and Christian leaders. There are at least four ways ILM can serve you:

1. Ministering to Ministry Leaders

ILM offers a unique two-day "Galatians 6:6" retreat to ministers and their spouses for personal renewal and for reestablishing and affirming ministry and family priorities. The conference accommodations and meals are provided as a gift to ministry leaders by cosponsoring partners. Thirty to forty such retreats are held throughout the U.S. and Europe each year.

2. Partnering with Denominations and Other Ministries

Numerous denominations and ministries have partnered with ILM by "commissioning" them to equip their ministry leaders through the Galatians 6:6 retreats along with strategic training and ongoing resources. This unique partnership enables a denomination to use the expertise of ILM trainers and resources to perpetuate a movement of Great Commandment ministry at the local level. ILM also provides a crisis-support setting where denominations may send ministers, couples, or families who are struggling in their relationships.

3. Identifying, Training, and Equipping Lay Leaders

ILM is committed to helping the church equip its lay leaders through:

- *Sermon Series* on several Great Commandment topics to help pastors communicate a vision for Great Commandment health as well as identify and cultivate a core lay leadership group.
- *Community Training Classes* that provide weekly or weekend training to church staff and lay leaders. Classes are delivered by Intimate Life trainers along with ILM video-assisted training, workbooks, and study courses.
- *One-Day Training Conferences* on implementing Great Commandment ministry in the local church through marriage, parenting, or singles ministry. Conducted by Intimate Life trainers, these conferences are a great way to jump-start Great Commandment ministry in a local church.

4. Providing Advanced Training and Crisis Support

ILM conducts advanced training for both ministry staff and lay leaders through the Leadership Institute, focusing on relational ministry (marriage, parenting, families, singles, men, women, blended families, and counseling). The Enrichment Center provides support to relationships in crisis through Intensive Retreats for couples, families, and singles.

For more information on how you, your church, or your denomination can take advantage of the many services and resources, such as the Great Commandment Ministry Training Resource offered by Intimate Life Ministries, write or call:

Intimate Life Ministries
P.O. Box 201808
Austin, TX 78720-1808
1-800-881-8008

Passing On the Truth to Our Next Generation

The Right From Wrong message, available in numerous formats, provides a blueprint for countering the culture and rebuilding the crumbling foundations of our families.

The Right From Wrong Book for Adults

Right From Wrong: What You Need to Know to Help Youth Make Right Choices
by Josh McDowell and Bob Hostetler

Our youth no longer live in a culture that teaches an objective standard of right and wrong. Truth has become a matter of taste. Morality has been replaced by individual preference. And today's youth have been affected. Fifty-seven percent of our churched youth cannot state that an objective standard of right and wrong even exists!

As the centerpiece of the Right From Wrong Campaign, this life-changing book provides you with a biblical, yet practical, blueprint for passing on core Christian values to the next generation.

Right From Wrong, Trade Paper Book
ISBN 0-8499-3604-7

The Truth Slayers Book for Youth

Truth Slayers: The Battle of Right From Wrong
by Josh McDowell and Bob Hostetler

This book, directed to youth, is written in the popular NovelPlus format. It combines the fascinating story of Brittney Marsh, Philip Milford, Jason Withers, and the consequences of their wrong choices with Josh McDowell's insights for young adults in sections called "The Inside Story."

Truth Slayers conveys the critical Right From Wrong message that challenges you to rely on God's Word as the absolute standard of truth in making right choices.

Truth Slayers, Trade Paper Book
ISBN 0-8499-3662-4

103 Questions Book for Children

103 Questions Children Ask about Right From Wrong
Introduction by Josh McDowell

"How does a person really know what is right or wrong?" "How does God decide what's wrong?" "If lying is wrong, why did God let some people in the Bible tell lies?" "What is a conscience and where does it come from?" These and 99 other questions are what kids ages 6 to 10 are asking. The *103 Questions* book equips parents to answer the tough questions kids ask about right from wrong. It also provides an easy-to-understand book that children will read and enjoy.

103 Questions, Trade Paper Book
ISBN 0-8423-4595-7

The Topsy-Turvy Kingdom Picture Book

The Topsy-Turvy Kingdom
by Dottie and Josh McDowell, with David Weiss

This fascinating story from a faraway land is written in delightful rhyme. It enables adults to teach children the importance of believing in and obeying an absolute standard of truth.

The Topsy-Turvy Kingdom, Hardcover Book for Children
ISBN 0-8423-7218-0

The Josh McDowell Family and Youth Devotionals

Josh McDowell's One Year Book of Youth Devotions by Bob Hostetler
Josh McDowell's One Year Book of Family Devotions by Bob Hostetler

These two devotionals may be used alone or together. Youth from ages 10 through 16 will enjoy the youth devotionals on their own. And they'll be able to participate in the family devotionals with their parents and siblings. Both devotionals are packed with fun-filled and inspiring readings. They will challenge you to think—and live—as "children of God without fault in a crooked and depraved generation, in which you shine like stars in the universe" (Philippians 2:15, NIV).

Josh McDowell's One Year Book of Youth Devotions
ISBN 0-8423-4301-6
Josh McDowell's One Year Book of Family Devotions
ISBN 0-8423-4302-4

Truth Matters,
Adult Video Series
ISBN 0-8499-8587-0

Setting Youth Free to Make Right
Choices, Youth Video Series
ISBN 0-8499-8585-4

Video Series for Adults and Youth

Truth Matters for You and Tomorrow's Generation Five-part adult video series featuring Josh McDowell
Setting Youth Free to Make Right Choices Five-part youth video series featuring Josh McDowell

These two interactive video series go beyond declaring what is right and wrong. They teach how to make right moral choices based on God's absolute standard of truth.

The adult series includes five video sessions, a comprehensive leader's guide with samplers from the five *Right From Wrong* workbooks, the *Right From Wrong* book, the *Truth Slayers* book, and an eight-minute promotional tape that will motivate adults to go through the series.

The youth series contains five video sessions, a leader's guide with reproducible handouts that include samplers from the *Right From Wrong* workbooks, and the *Truth Slayers* book.

The Right From Wrong Musicals for Youth

Truth Works musical by Dennis and Nan Allen
Truth Slayers musical by Steven V. Taylor and Matt Tullos

The *Truth Slayers* musical for junior high and high school students is based on the *Truth Slayers* book. The *Truth Works* musical for children is based on the *Truth Works* workbooks. As youth and children perform these musicals for their peers and families, they have a unique opportunity to tell of the life-changing message of Right From Wrong.

Each musical includes complete leader's instructions, a songbook of all music used, a dramatic script, and an accompanying sound track on cassette or compact disc.

Truth Works,
Musical Score
Number 318004
Truth Slayers,
Musical Score
Number 314002

Workbook for Adults

Truth Matters for You and Tomorrow's Generation
Workbook and Leader's Guide
by Josh McDowell

The *Truth Matters* workbook includes 35 daily activities that help you to instill within your children and youth such biblical values as honesty, love, and sexual purity. By taking just 25 to 30 minutes each day, you will discover a fresh and effective way to teach your family how to make right choices—even in tough situations.

The *Truth Matters* workbook is designed to be used in eight adult group sessions that encourage interaction and support building. The five daily activities between each group meeting will help you and your family make right choices a habit.

Truth Matters,
Member's Workbook
ISBN 0-8054-9834-6
Truth Matters, Leader's Guide
ISBN 0-8054-9833-8

Workbook for College Students

Out of the Moral Maze, Workbook with Leader's Instructions
by Josh McDowell

Students entering college face a culture that has lost its belief in absolutes. In today's society, truth is a matter of taste; morality, a matter of individual preference. *Out of the Moral Maze* will provide any truth-seeking collegian with a sound moral guidance system based on God and his Word as the determining factors for making right moral choices.

Out of the Moral Maze
Member's Workbook and Leader's Instructions
ISBN 0-8054-9832-X

Workbook for Junior High and High School Students

Setting You Free to Make Right Choices
Workbook and Leader's Guide
by Josh McDowell

With a Bible-based emphasis, this workbook creatively and systematically teaches your students how to determine right from wrong in their everyday lives—specifically applying the decision-making process to moral questions about lying, cheating, getting even, and premarital sex.

Through eight youth-group meetings, followed each week by five daily exercises of 20 to 25 minutes per day, your teenagers will be challenged to develop a lifelong habit of making right moral choices.

Setting You Free to Make Right Choices,
Member's Workbook ISBN 0-8054-9828-1
Setting You Free to Make Right Choices,
Leader's Guide ISBN 0-8054-9829-X

Workbooks for Children

Truth Works: Making Right Choices
Workbooks and Leader's Guide
by Josh McDowell

To pass on the truth and reclaim a generation, we must teach God's truth when our children's minds and hearts are young and pliable. Creatively developed, *Truth Works* includes two workbooks, one directed to younger children in grades one to three, the other to older children in grades four to six.

In eight fun-filled group sessions, your children will discover why such truths as honesty, justice, love, purity, self-control, mercy, and respect work to their best interests. They will see how four simple steps will help them make right moral choices an everyday habit.

Truth Works, Younger Children's Workbook ISBN 0-8054-9831-1
Truth Works, Older Children's Workbook ISBN 0-8054-9830-3
Truth Works, Leader's Guide ISBN 0-8054-9827-3

Contact your Christian supplier to help you obtain these Right From Wrong resources, and begin to make it right in your home, your church, and your community.

About the Author

Josh McDowell is an internationally known speaker, author, and traveling representative of Campus Crusade for Christ. A graduate of Wheaton College and Talbot Theological Seminary, Josh has authored more than forty-five books, including *More Than a Carpenter*, *Evidence That Demands a Verdict*, and *Right from Wrong*. Josh and his wife, Dottie, have four children and live in Lucas, Texas.